Organic
OUTREACH
FOR FAMILIES

Other Books in the Organic Outreach Series

Organic Outreach for Ordinary People

Organic Outreach for Churches

Other Books by Kevin and Sherry Harney

Leadership from the Inside Out

Seismic Shifts

*Finding a Church You Can Love and
Loving the Church You've Found*

The U-Turn Church

Reckless Faith

Small Group Resources

Interactions Small Group Series (with Bill Hybels)

New Community Small Group Series (with Bill Hybels, John Ortberg)

John: An Intimate Look at the Savior

Ephesians: Bringing Heaven to Earth

Sacred Marriage (with Gary Thomas)

Divine Conspiracy (with Dallas Willard)

Real Women, Real Faith, volumes 1–2

God's Story, Your Story (with Max Lucado)

Circle Maker (with Mark Batterson)

Undaunted (with Christine Caine)

Curriculum and Church Resources

Old Testament Challenge (with John Ortberg)

This We Believe

The Story for Groups (with Randy Frazee)

Organic OUTREACH

FOR FAMILIES

TURNING YOUR HOME INTO A LIGHTHOUSE

Kevin G. Harney
& Sherry Harney

ZONDERVAN®

ZONDERVAN.com/
AUTHORTRACKER
follow your favorite authors

We want to hear from you. Please send your comments about this book to us in care of zreview@zondervan.com. Thank you.

ZONDERVAN

Organic Outreach for Families
Copyright © 2012 by Kevin G. Harney and Sherry Harney

This title is also available as a Zondervan ebook.
Visit www.zondervan.com/ebooks.

Requests for information should be addressed to:

Zondervan, *Grand Rapids, Michigan 49530*

Library of Congress Cataloging-in-Publication Data

Harney, Kevin.
    Organic outreach for families: turning your home into a lighthouse / Kevin G. Harney and Sherry Harney.
        p. cm.
    Includes bibliographical references.
    ISBN 978-0-310-27397-4 (pbk.)
        1. Home—Religious aspects—Christianity. 2. Families—Religious life. 3. Hospitality—Religious aspects—Christianity. 4. Evangelistic work. I. Harney, Sherry, 1960- II. Title.
    BR115.H56H37 2012
    248'.5—dc23   2012018872

Cover design: *Jay Smith/Juicebox Design*
Interior design: *Ben Fetterley/Matthew Van Zomeren*

Printed in the United States of America

---

15 16 17 18 /DCI/ 20 19 18 17 16 15 14 13 12 11 10 9 8 7 6 5 4 3 2

Contents

Acknowledgments

We give special thanks and recognition to our three sons, Zach, Josh, and Nate. Not only have they lived every page of this book but they have joyfully and prayerfully engaged in organic outreach as partners with us. As an added bonus, they each contributed three pieces to this book. We are honored to call each of you our sons.

To all of our friends on Richfield Court, living near you for seventeen years was a joy beyond words. We laughed, prayed, cried, ate (amazing meals!), played, and watched our families grow up together. We saw God's presence and grace fill our lives, homes, cul-de-sac, and community. We love each of you.

To Lee Strobel and Mark Mittelberg, for years you have both encouraged us to write this book. Thank you for your prayers, encouragement, friendship, and partnership in the gospel for almost two decades.

To the team at Zondervan, our twenty years of collaboration have been a privilege. Your partnership in ministry and life means more than you know.

Ryan Pazdur, you have traveled the entire three-book journey of organic outreach with us, and by God's providence you have spent many years being a part of our family and community. You have seen organic outreach up close and personal. We have been blessed by you more than words can say. Thank you for leveraging your keen intellect and passionate heart for outreach.

Brian Phipps, your editorial expertise strengthens everything we write. The past decade of our publishing partnership has been a joy. Thanks for giving every book your full attention.

Andrew Rogers, your skill at getting the message of organic outreach out to the church and the world is a blessing. Thank you for using your gifts to move believers into the world with the good news of Jesus Christ.

Introduction

A Light in the Darkness

Let your light shine before others, that they may see your
good deeds and glorify your Father in heaven.

— Matthew 5:16

Many of us are missing something in life because we are
after the second best. I put before you what I have found
to be the best — one who is worthy of all our devotion —
Jesus Christ. He is the Saviour for the young and the old.
Lord, here I am.

*— Eric Liddell, Olympic gold medalist
and missionary to China*

Over the past thirty years, **Sherry** and I have lived in all sorts of
places. We've lived in an apartment, a trailer, a triplex (in a very
rough neighborhood), a townhouse, a parsonage, and a house. Though
each structure was different, we observed one thing that remained constant: it isn't the type of home but the people in it that make a difference. It is through the residents, not the structure, that God shines his
light in the darkness. Our prayer and desire has been the same in each
place we have lived: "Lord, let your light so fill our hearts and home that
it shines into the community around us." Wherever God puts us, we
want people to see the face of Jesus and experience his grace in natural
and organic ways. This has happened in each place we have lived.

Every house, apartment, trailer, military residence, townhome,
duplex, triplex, and condominium can be a lighthouse of God's presence

and grace. God dreams of this. Jesus died for this. The living God longs for his presence and power to be on display, shining brightly, in your neighborhood. The fact that you are reading this book says something about your heart. It beats with God's heart. You want your home to be attractive to others, a beacon of Christ-honoring influence.

Homes are not the only place where God shines his light. God plants churches all over the world to reflect his love and exhibit his amazing grace.[1] He also sends his people into the world to bring his message of salvation to the lost, broken, and hurting.[2] You can find plenty of books (including some that we have written) that aim to help you and your church become a more effective witness. What is often overlooked and forgotten is God's design for every Christian home to be a lighthouse. The average home can be the place where people discover what only the Savior can bring.

Living in a neighborhood presents a strategic opportunity to be a witness of God's grace. People see you come and go. They watch how you live. Neighbors hear how you talk to your spouse and kids. They see how you spend your time together. Living in close proximity creates an atmosphere where the Holy Spirit can move and do beautiful things. God wants people to be drawn to our homes because they are outposts of his grace, joy, hope, truth, and love in a world that hungers for all of these things. In this dark world there is a profound need for light, and when light shines in the darkness, people are drawn to it. Like a warm campfire on a cold and pitch-black night, people can't help but come near. When you add in some hot cocoa and s'mores, it's irresistible!

OUR STORY

My wife, Sherry, and I come from very different backgrounds. Sherry grew up in a family with strong Christian roots. She went to church twice every Sunday and attended Sunday school faithfully. She regularly attended youth group events. Each Wednesday, Sherry's family gathered with God's people to study the Bible and encourage one another. Church activities were a valuable part of her life, and Sherry was often the last person to leave church because she so enjoyed the connection with other believers. She was hungry to learn the things of God.

I, on the other hand, grew up outside the church, with no faith framework or understanding of God. I lived in a loving and caring home, but we did not go to church, talk about God, or pray before meals, and we certainly did not recognize Jesus as our Savior. Faith was not even an ancillary part of our lives. God was a nonissue. Yet by God's amazing grace, I heard the message of the gospel and was saved by Jesus during my high school years. I became active in sharing my faith and soon had a growing desire not only to follow Christ but to teach others to do the same.

When Sherry and I first met, in 1982, we shared this common passion for people to know the amazing grace of God, the life-changing gospel of Jesus, and the tender filling of the Holy Spirit. We married in 1984, and from the start we were unified in our vision to do all we could to let the light of Jesus shine in and through us, wherever we lived. Almost ten years into our marriage, God clarified this vision even further. We began to understand that the Holy Spirit uses ordinary people right where they live to shine his light in the darkness. So we prayed in very specific ways that our home would become a beacon of God's light and would shine in our community to draw people to Jesus. We found we had a new passion for our neighbors to know the love and grace of God.

That vision and passion led to a three-book series on what we refer to as "organic outreach." The first book, *Organic Outreach for Ordinary People*, focuses on how your personal lifestyle and journey of faith present natural opportunities for sharing God's message of love with the people around you.[3] I wrote it to help ordinary people — not just the highly evangelistic, confrontational types — learn to communicate and share the extraordinary message of the gospel. The concept of organic outreach is based on the conviction that we can share the love, grace, and message of Jesus in ways that feel natural for us, regardless of our personality type, life experience, or skill set, and we can learn to connect with the people around us right where they are. Organic outreach is not a program that every person follows the same way. It is an understanding of faith and life that releases every believer to share the love and message of Jesus in a way that feels right for them.

In *Organic Outreach for Churches*, I develop the vision of sharing the good news of the Savior in natural ways through the local church.[4] Sadly, some congregations choose to circle the wagons, hunker down, and protect their turf. They do all they can to keep the world from getting in. But this is not God's divine design. He wants every church to become a mighty force for God in its community and beyond.

This book, *Organic Outreach for Families*, shows what God's call to share our faith in natural, organic ways means in the context of the home. It's a book we've written to help ordinary families, like yours, make a God-honoring impact right where he has placed you. We write from personal experience, so most of our examples and illustrations involve families with parents and children living at home. But while the ideas and concepts are primarily directed at families, the content will also be helpful for newly married couples, empty nesters, and any Christian who wants their home to be a place where the light of God's grace shines.

THE JOURNEY AHEAD OF US

This book is structured in three sections. The first section focuses on helping parents reach their children and extended family with the love and truth of Jesus. You will find practical tools to point your family members toward the Savior in natural, effective, and fun ways. If you are a grandparent, these chapters will also help you to communicate the love and grace of Jesus to your grandchildren. We believe that before we can be a lighthouse of God's grace, we must know how to bring the truth and friendship of Jesus to the people closest to us. If this is where you are in your journey, begin in section one.

The next section digs a bit deeper into the importance of raising children who don't merely receive the light of Jesus but who let it shine through them. We can't just share the good news with our kids, watch them enter a relationship with Jesus, and think our job is done. We need to help our children enter into the work of the Great Commission, discipling them and teaching them how to share their faith with others. Jesus was clear about this when he said, "Therefore go and make disciples of all nations, baptizing them in the name of the Father and of the Son and of the Holy Spirit, and teaching them to obey everything I have commanded you. And surely I am with you always, to the very end of the age."⁵ Jesus promised that we will be empowered to do what he commanded, saying, "You will receive power when the Holy Spirit comes on you; and you will be my witnesses in Jerusalem, and in all Judea and Samaria, and to the ends of the earth."⁶ Jesus gave his final directives to his followers through these powerfully instructive moments after his resurrection and before he ascended to heaven, and we believe these commands should be the passionate cry of our children's hearts, even from their youngest days. God desires that our homes be incubators of spiritual health and maturity, and this includes developing an evangelistic passion in our children.

The final section of the book explores how to transform your home into a lighthouse of God's love and grace. The homes we live in can become attractive locations for children, teens, and other adults. God wants to use us to give others a bearing in the storms of life, a point of reference that helps them change direction, like a lighthouse that keeps ships from crashing on dangerous shores. A lighthouse, ultimately, guides people into a safe harbor. In this section, we'll consider ways our home can help people come in from the storm-filled world and find rest, hope, and a safe haven in Jesus Christ. We'll look at practical ways families can live, love, serve, and speak with grace. We will also look at how to go into our community and bring the gospel of Jesus to people right where they are. It's not enough to shine our light and hope people will notice it and be drawn to our home to meet Jesus. Some may come, but many will not. So we also need to be ready to go out, to meet people where they are.

YOUR HOME, A BEACON OF GOD'S LIGHT

What does it look like for your home to be a beacon of God's presence in your neighborhood and community? We want to begin by clarifying that it will look a little different for each of us. What images come to your mind? Perhaps a place for people to stop in unannounced, where they know they are welcome at any time? Maybe you picture a comfortable space where others can sit for a leisurely dinner? Or a location where conversations about life and God are normal and natural? Somewhere folks can stop, take a deep breath, and relax? A spot where someone can unload their burdens? A location where they can sit by some flowers or a quiet pond, feel a gentle breeze, or see a beautiful sunset? Maybe you picture a place where people can laugh until it hurts or cry until they are out of tears?

Every lighthouse home will look a bit different, but they will all have one thing in common. They will be places where Jesus is King, where his love is present, and where the Holy Spirit is at work. A lighthouse home is a place where the amazing grace of God is felt and the saving message of Jesus is heard. It's a place where the glow of God's light is strong and people are drawn to the Savior. Homes like this can change a community, a state, and a nation, even the world.

If you are interested in having a home like this, in praying with fresh boldness and loving others with grace, this book was written for you. We've filled it with stories and examples from our own experience, but we've also made it a toolbox of practical ideas that you can adapt to your home and community right away. Before you begin, though, we encourage you to brace yourself. When you commit your home to God, you must be prepared for what will happen when God shows up. He will always do something far beyond your wildest dreams. This is an adventure that can begin today, and it will last the rest of your life. Trust us, you will no longer be satisfied with seeing your home as simply a place to live. Your heart will quickly be captured by the vision of being a shining light of God's presence in a dark and desperate world. Let the adventure begin!

Part One

REACHING YOUR OWN FAMILY

Something is very wrong if we reach our neighbors with the love of Jesus but our children feel forgotten and marginalized. We have confused our priorities if we invest more time in our church than we do in our own children. Our first priority as parents is to love, teach, and lead our children toward an authentic and life-changing relationship with the Savior.

Jesus called his followers to be his witnesses to the very ends of the earth, but he also told them to start right where they lived (Acts 1:8). This section is a reminder that God calls us to reach our family with the love, grace, and message of Jesus Christ *before* we turn our attention to our neighbors and community.

Chapter One

Living the Gospel in Your Home

Kevin

Hear, O Israel: The LORD our God, the LORD is one. Love the LORD your God with all your heart and with all your soul and with all your strength. These commandments that I give you today are to be on your hearts. Impress them on your children. Talk about them when you sit at home and when you walk along the road, when you lie down and when you get up.
— *Deuteronomy 6:4-7*

I have but one passion: It is He, it is He alone. The world is the field and the field is the world; and henceforth that country shall be my home where I can be most used in winning souls for Christ.
— *Count Nikolaus Ludwig von Zinzendorf*

As a junior in college and a fairly new follower of Christ, I was excited to be moving to the Midwest to attend a Christian school filled with passionate, committed, and excited young believers. I had attended only public schools before, and so I arrived at my new college with great enthusiasm.

As I got to know my fellow students, however, I was shocked to discover that many of them were angry with their parents and hostile toward God. I spent time listening to young men and women who had grown up in a pastor's home or were raised on the mission field. Often, they were resentful of, not excited about, the Christian faith. To be fair, some of the finest young people I have ever known attended this school. They loved Jesus, and they longed to share the good news of the Savior with others. But they were the exception. An overwhelming number of the students were either hostile toward God or apathetic about the gospel. Some had been "forced" to attend this school because it was the alma mater of their parents and grandparents. Some admitted that they were not even sure if they believed in God or the Bible. Others assented to the Christian faith but seemed indifferent to growing in their faith.

I had expected a campus teeming with students who were excited and committed followers of Jesus. I assumed my classmates would be thankful for the chance to attend such a great Christian school. I thought they would be hungry to be equipped to bring the good news of Jesus to the world.

I was wrong.

I was disturbed each time I met a student who was hurt, angry, or apathetic about their faith. I found myself wondering why some kids who grew up in strong Christian homes ended up far from God.

During that year of college, my future wife, Sherry, was living two thousand miles away in California. We talked on the phone once a week (this was before cell phones, text messaging, email, and Skype), and I learned that she had also encountered people who were raised in Christian families but had wandered from the faith. We talked about these encounters and began praying about the home environment we wanted our family to have when we were married. We discussed how we did not want our kids to end up bitter, resentful, and cynical toward God. Even while we were dating, we were praying and thinking about how we could raise our kids to know and love Jesus.

Keep in mind that we did not have a tight and orderly child-rearing program worked out to guarantee that our children would grow up to love God. When we got married, we had some goals and dreams, but we lacked a parenting "system" to make them a reality. And we admit, now that all three of our sons are adults, that we still do not have a nice tidy scheme to guarantee that kids will grow to follow Jesus with a heart of love for God. We all know it's just not that simple.

Still, the years of marriage and parenting have taught us some healthy and practical guidelines that are biblical and easily transferable. We did not turn our home into a mini seminary. Nor did we build a fortress to keep our kids trapped inside. We made no effort to dig a moat around our home to keep the weirdness and evil of the world out. We did not do nightly Bible memory programs and drill our kids endlessly about what book comes after Ezekiel or how many chapters are in 2 Corinthians. We did not force our kids to attend every church activity and behave differently from their peers. We raised them to believe in Jesus and love him with sincere hearts. We sought to model a hunger for Scripture and passion for prayer. We lived our faith as an open book and invited them into the joy and journey of walking with Jesus.

Today, all three of our adult sons have authentic friendships with Jesus. They love the church, and each of them enjoys participating in the life of a congregation by using his gifts to serve God and others. They are passionate about sharing the gospel with friends, family, and the world. Each of our sons feels called to Christian service through the church, the mission field, or the arts. In the pages ahead, you'll hear from them from time to time as they share glimpses of what it was like to grow up in a home where their parents sought to make their home a lighthouse of God's grace.

REAL FAITH

We can't give others what we don't have. If we want our children to love Jesus with authentic and passionate hearts, we, as parents, must have a living and dynamic relationship with God. This isn't about being "religious." It's about loving the one true God of the Bible, who reveals himself as Father, Son, and Holy Spirit. Parents who are lukewarm about living for God can't expect their kids to shine brightly for Jesus. Dropping our kids off at church events so they can get a weekly dose of God isn't enough. We need to examine our own relationship with God and ask, If my child grows up to have a faith like mine, would that be a good thing?

The idea of "organic outreach" begins with a personal friendship with God through faith in Jesus. The faith of parents who are growing in their love for God is contagious, spreading throughout their home. Because their faith is real, it permeates their lives. We must live the gospel in our homes before we can share it in the world. We can't expect our children to have a deep relationship with Jesus if ours is shallow.

FRIENDSHIP WITH JESUS

When your children look at you, do they see a friend of Jesus? Do they hear you talk about God with affection and joy? Do your kids see evidence that the Holy Spirit is alive and at work in your heart? I made sure to tell my boys when they were young that I loved God even more than I loved them. They were surprised to hear me say this at first. Then I told them that I loved God even more than I loved their mom. That really shocked them, because they knew how crazy I was about their mother! I explained that I can be a good dad and husband only if I love God first and walk close to Jesus. When I am not following Jesus, I am not the husband and father I want to be.

Today, if you ask any of our three sons, Zach, Josh, and Nate, who their parents love most in the world, they will tell you that both Sherry and I love God more than anyone, including them. Knowing this actually brings them comfort. Our sons have watched their mom closely their entire lives. They have seen a woman who loves God. They have seen how whenever they had a concern, their mother responded to them with faith and turned to Jesus for help. They saw the example of parents who look to Scripture for guidance and regularly pray for wisdom. They learned that a home can be a lighthouse to others only when it is connected to the one who is the source of all light and life.

PASSION FOR THE BIBLE AS GOD'S TRUTH

Parents who want to see their children grow strong in their faith need to love God's Word and regularly read the Bible. In our world, moral absolutes are questioned, and the Bible is mocked. Our children need to learn that God has clearly spoken in the Bible and has told us how we can enjoy a relationship with him. Our words and actions should model for our kids what it's like to dig into the Word and build our lives on its teaching.

What does this look like? Rather than giving you our perspective, we asked our oldest son, Zach, for his answer to that question. At the time he wrote this, Zach was twenty-four years old and serving in a church full-time while attending seminary. We asked him to share his perspective on these two questions: How can parents help their kids grow in knowledge of the Bible? How can parents foster a lifelong commitment to reading and studying God's Word?

RAISING CHILDREN IN A POSTMODERN WORLD
Zach Harney

If you are currently raising children, they are being raised in a postmodern world. If you plan on raising children anytime soon, they will also be raised in a postmodern world. But what is postmodernism? It sounds like an improvement or more advanced version of modernism. But more specifically, what is it? To truly describe what it means would take more room than even this entire book has to offer, because it permeates architecture, literature, pop culture, and almost every facet of life, and it means something a little bit different in each area. Without getting into extremely specific and technical jargon, I will try to illuminate why it is important in leading a family and raising Christian children.

Professor and author Elizabeth Wilson says, "Postmodernism refuses to privilege any one perspective, and recognizes only difference, never inequality, only fragments, never conflict." What this means is that postmodern people do not believe that one perspective is better than another. They believe that opinions, no matter how different they are from each other, should never conflict with another, because our viewpoints are only a matter of opinion. What is good for one person may not be good for another. As long as laws are not being broken and people are not being hurt, a person should be able to live the way they want, because one person's truth is not necessarily another person's truth.

This viewpoint is rooted in a process of history. Humanity has been trying to find answers to life's biggest questions since the beginning of the world. An attempt to find truth has existed for thousands of years, but postmodernism is a sign of giving up this search, or, in the minds of postmodernists, an awakening to the complex world of relative truth. In their minds, religion has failed to provide an all-encompassing explanation of the world. On the other hand, the hard sciences also have failed to provide truth that explains or validates why we exist. If religion and science have failed to produce a system of truth, then it can only be found in each individual. Postmodernists believe that truth is relative, which means that no one viewpoint is correct; it is simply what is "right" for that individual.

The main problem with this, though, is that we are a fallen people with really messed up desires and minds. Without some sort of objective morality or all-encompassing truth, we can get into a lot of trouble by simply following what "feels right" for us. This is the world that we live in, it is the world I grew up in, and there is no getting around it. In this world, we are taught from a young age to be tolerant of everything, as long as it does not cause us physical harm or infringe on a very loose definition of our rights. Most of the time it is subconscious; it has permeated the minds of many young people without their having any idea that it is engrained in their minds. I realize this when someone older than me calls something that seems harmless "sin" or says that something is "wrong." Something deep inside of me responds, "You can't tell me what is right and wrong; that's just what *you* believe." The trouble with this viewpoint is that there are things that are right and wrong, at least if you believe that the Bible is, as 2 Timothy 3:16 says, "God-breathed and is useful for teaching, rebuking, correcting and training in righteousness."

This is why one of the greatest things that a parent can do is teach their child to read and understand the Word of God. Unless a young person is committed to reading and believing Scripture, they will inevitably be heavily influenced by the culture of postmodernism and relative truth. Much of American society, especially the younger generations, already buys into this, and it has infused itself in most secular institutions, the general media, literature, and even many Christian institutions. It is rooted in a falling away from scriptural truths. The Bible clearly teaches, over and over again, that there are things that aren't permissible by God and that by committing these actions or having certain attitudes, we are going against his desire for us. Without some sort of guidepost, we are blindly stumbling in the exact same way that everyone else is. The most effective response of a parent who wants their child to be a light, someone who reaches out to the lost people around them, is not only to model what a Christian acts like on a day-to-day basis but to prepare them with Scripture for a confused world. Without this preparation, they will be just as lost as the next person, and when someone who is spiritually curious comes to them with questions, they won't have the definitive answers that come from God's truth. They will give the same conjecture and uncertainty as everyone else does.

When my brothers and I were kids, our parents tried every possible thing they could to get us to read the Bible. My father would make us comprehensive reading guides with some sort of reward at the end. Every time we went on a vacation, we read through a book of the Bible (usually a smaller one). For a while, we were each asked to do our own devotion, and then we would meet once a week to talk about it. My parents would always get us the type of Bible that we wanted. (My favorite was the NIV Archaeological Study Bible.) Some of the incentives lasted a long time, and at other times, we would slow down in our Bible reading, but it was always seen as important.

Probably the greatest service they did for us was not shoving it down our throats. Though it was greatly encouraged, it was never forced, and while we may not have read the Bible as much as we could have, our love for the Bible continued to grow. In fact, all three of us were involved in some sort of biblical study in our education, and in recent years, the Bible has become more alive and interesting than I could ever have imagined. I saw my parents reading the Bible every day because they loved it, and this was often a mystery to me as a young child, but now I know I will be passing the same legacy on to my children through encouragement and example.

A PLACE OF GRACE

The message of the gospel is grace to the core. The apostle Paul put it this way: "For it is by grace you have been saved, through faith—and this is not from yourselves, it is the gift of God—not by works, so that no one can boast."[1] The gift of Jesus, his death on the cross, the payment for our sins, the glory of the resurrection—none of these are earned or deserved. They are gifts of grace. God knows all about our sin, and yet he entered human history to die for us anyway. "But God demonstrates his own love for us in this: While we were still sinners, Christ died for us."[2] A lighthouse home is a place that radiates this grace, and it begins with the way parents raise their children.

Parents live the gospel in their home as they are daily reminded of the undeserved grace and mercy God has shown by forgiving their sin and failure. Parents who have received grace can humbly walk in grace. As this happens, they can freely extend grace to others, beginning with their children. This doesn't mean that dads and moms should not be firm and consistent with discipline when it is needed. Grace is not about spoiling kids, nor is it opposed to discipline and correction. Rather, it is quick to forgive, committed to restoration, and lavish with kindness and love. It is a love that is based on what is good, right, and true, yet it is motivated by mercy and a deep awareness of our need for God's saving help through Jesus. Our children should be reminded on a regular basis that they are loved by God, precious in his sight, and valued more than they dream.

Grace rules a home when parents tell stories of how they have received the forgiveness of Jesus and model that same love by forgiving their children. Parents set an example for their children when they repeat the story of their conversion, sharing the gospel with their kids, again and again, with awestruck humility. Parents inspire their children to seek God when they talk freely about how God loves, guides, helps, and forgives them, all in the normal flow of everyday life.

You know that God's grace has permeated a family when parents can admit their own frailties, faults, and foibles to their kids and rejoice with them that they are saved by grace alone. Sherry and I both have experienced moments when we handled something poorly with our boys and had to ask them for forgiveness. These became sacred moments as our boys discovered that parents need grace too. Children understand grace as their parents forgive them quickly, not holding grudges or reminding them of failures. Parents should graciously remind their kids that God has dealt with their disobedience and sin on the cross. We don't hold our children's mistakes over their heads. When they admit their mistakes and confess them, we model the love of God and treat them as people who have been cleansed by the blood of Jesus.

The culture of a home also reflects grace when parents refuse to speak judgmental words about people in their community, church, or extended family. If we have sharp tongues and critical spirits in the privacy of our homes, our children soon recognize our hypocrisy. We can declare that we live in the love of God, but our words are a compelling witness that the gospel of grace does not yet rule in our hearts and homes.

In the coming chapters, we will look at some practical ways our family members can experience the presence of Jesus and the power of his grace within the walls of our homes. The starting point is recognizing that we can't give what we don't have. If we want our homes to be lighthouses of God's grace, it begins with us, with our grasp of the gospel of God's grace and our walk with the Lord. As we walk with Jesus, revel in his grace, long for him to be glorified, and delight in our friendship with the Savior, we naturally bring this good news to the most important people in our lives, our children.

BECOMING A
LIGHTHOUSE

Try one of these ideas in your home and with your family ...

Talk about It. Plan a family meal and make the topic of discussion these three questions:

1. How are the love and grace of Jesus being experienced inside the walls of our home?
2. How could we show the grace of Jesus more fully as we live with each other in our home?
3. When people outside our home look at our family, in what ways can they see the presence and love of Jesus?

The Friendship Factor. Like it or not, your children are watching you all the time, whether they are five years old, fifteen, or twenty-five. They follow your cues and emulate your lifestyle. Reflect on these two questions: (1) What are some of the ways my children can see that I have a real and growing friendship with God? (2) What are one or two ways I can deepen and grow my relationship with Jesus? In the coming week, seek to go deeper with God, and let your kids know you are taking this step of faith.

Truth Source. Healthy homes are built on the truth of the Bible. In a world of radical relativism and moral flexibility, our families need to be established on the solid rock of Jesus and his Word. Begin now to encourage your children to read the Bible. Remember that their best motivation is seeing you reading God's Word and hearing you talk about what you are learning. When they see transformation in your life, they will hunger for it too.

Resources for Parents. Here are a few ideas to help you help your children to grow to love the Bible:

- *The Story* is an amazing resource. It is a chronological compilation of biblical passages that teaches the whole story of the Bible in thirty-one easy-to-read chapters. As a bonus, it includes materials for children, teens, and adults. Learn more about this resource at *http://www.thestory.com/home.*
- *The Adventure Bible Handbook* is a resource we spent countless evenings reading with our boys. The artwork, format, and content were compelling to them and even to us as parents.
- Let your children pick out a Bible that really connects for them. This can be a fun time of bonding, talking about the various study Bibles, topical Bibles, and age-appropriate Bibles that are available today.

Chapter Two

Sharing Jesus with Your Children

Sherry

Blessed are those who fear the LORD, who find great delight in his commands. Their children will be mighty in the land; the generation of the upright will be blessed.

— Psalm 112:1 - 2

I am ready to burn out for God. I am ready to endure any hardship, if by any means I might save some. The longing of my heart is to make known my glorious Redeemer to those who have never heard.

— William Burns

We have a great video of our youngest son, Nate, during his first swimming lesson, when he was just three years old. In the video he excitedly talks about his new adventure before wading into the water. The look on his face says it all — this moment is much bigger than he realized! He nervously jokes with us, not sure what lies ahead. The next scene captures our sweet little boy trying to focus and listen to his instructor, but you can see his eyes dart toward the water every few seconds. You can tell that he is on the verge of tears. He's not sure he wants to do this now, and he's beginning to realize that this whole adventure of learning to swim is going to be harder—and scarier—than he thought. The last scene is Nate in the water, pulling and kicking for all he is worth. He finally makes it to the side of the pool, and as he lifts his head out of the water, Nate looks at the camera. With a strained and somewhat desperate cry he asks, "Am I done yet?"

Parenting is a lot like learning to swim. You begin with pent up excitement and can hardly wait. Then you are thrown into the deep end of the parenting pool and find yourself fighting for air, crying to God for help. Parenting is bigger and scarier than you ever imagined. You constantly wonder, "Am I done yet?" only to realize afresh that it is a lifetime journey. You are just getting warmed up.

We found that parenting was more complex than we had assumed it would be when we first got married because it involves the spiritual training of children. We soon learned that though each of our children is "fearfully and wonderfully made," they are all so different.[1] There is no one-size-fits-all formula or a manual with clear directions for raising children. We need wisdom that is greater than any of us possess.

RAISE A CHILD TO LOVE JESUS

Growing up in the church, I often heard this verse quoted: "Train up a child in the way he should go; even when he is old he will not depart from it."[2] The interpretation people gave was fairly simple. Raise your child in the church, teach them the Bible, model faith in the home, and that child will eventually embrace the Christian faith, even if they have a time of rebellion. When I became a mother, this was the way I understood the passage as well.

Over twenty years ago Kevin and I began writing and editing books and Bible studies, and one of the first projects I worked on was a book by Chuck Swindoll[3] titled *The Strong Family*. In this book Swindoll expounds on the meaning of that important and familiar verse on raising children, and he brings some fresh exegetical insight to it.[4] Swindoll explains how the words "train up a child" point us to several helpful images. The first is a rope attached to a bit in a horse's mouth. The rope is used to turn the horse's head so that it moves in the right direction and learns to follow the rider's lead. This image is about guiding a child to learn to follow the lead of another. The second image is an ancient Hebrew midwife crushing grapes and rubbing them in a newborn's mouth to stimulate a sucking response. This image is about creating a desire for the things that give and maintain life. Swindoll points out that when we train up our children, we must do both of these. We point them in the right direction—one that honors God—and teach them to follow his leading and guidance. But we also seek to create a desire in them, a longing for the things that lead to health and life.

In other words, training children is so much more than just pounding information into their minds that they can regurgitate on demand. It's more than requiring them to attend every church event. The heart of training is direction and desire: helping a child discover the direction God has called them and teaching them to desire the things that honor God and bring the greatest joy in life.

The second phrase—"in the way he should go"—points to a child learning to be who God designed them to be. A helpful image here is a soaring eagle.[5] Have you ever felt the breathtaking awe of watching an eagle glide through the sky? The way an eagle moves is simply eagle-like. It is unique, as is the way a snake moves on a rock, the way a ship sails on the high seas, and the way a man is with a woman.[6] Each one of these pictures is distinct and recognizable.

If our goal is to raise children of light in this dark world, we need to help our sons and daughters become the unique and wonderful people God designed them to be. We can't try to mass-produce cookie-cutter kids who all look and act the same. We must not try to force our children into the mold of what we think a good Christian child should look like. We must get to know their God-given distinctives and their particular bents in order to help them become the person who God wants them to be. We believe this honors God and our children.

The final part of this verse says, "Even when he is old he will not depart from it." Swindoll observes that "old" doesn't refer to an elderly man. It refers to a time in life when boys begin growing facial hair, the season of puberty when our sons and daughters move into adulthood.

The point is clear: the primary time parents have to influence and guide the direction of their children is when they are growing up in our homes.

After reading Swindoll's insights, Kevin and I had a whole new picture of this passage and what it means to raise children. We understood that parenting is about more than simply getting our children to church and teaching them some basic biblical truths in the hope that they will come around to God's way when they get older. Rather, we were encouraged to study our children and get to know them so that we could help them follow God in a way that fits who they are. As our children grew toward adulthood, we sought to help them become the person of faith God designed them to be, not the person we thought they should be. We focused on their hearts, asking questions and guiding their desires for God in appropriate ways so that they would reach their God-given potential, longing to walk with Jesus and grow in faith in ways that feel natural to them.

At the time I first read this interpretation of the passage, I had hit a parenting roadblock. I was trying to raise our second son to be just like our first, and it wasn't working. My default parenting methods had worked just fine for our firstborn, Zach, but that same style and approach was just not working with Josh. I was frustrated, and so was he! Thankfully, a fresh understanding from Proverbs and Chuck Swindoll led to a significant shift.

Instead of using the same parenting style with both boys, I began to look at Josh as a uniquely created child of God. I realized that I needed to grow and learn just as much as Josh did. I needed to get to know my son better so that I could effectively train him in a way that would allow him to become all that God desired for him. I stopped forcing onto him my preconceived notions of who he should be and trusted that God would lead the way. I knew that because God created my son, he knows my son's future much better than I ever could. God alone knows the contribution he wants each of our children to make in this world for his glory. As we began raising all three of our boys in this new way, their love for God, church, the Bible, and the world grew.

Looking back, we realize that the key was not another formula or system for helping our kids come to faith in Jesus. Instead, it was understanding that the best way to parent our children is to get to know them. We began to watch them closely, talk with them, and discover their unique, God-given way of thinking and being. This takes a lot of time and energy. It's not a simple methodology or a five-step program, but it is worth it!

CELEBRATE EACH CHILD'S UNIQUENESS

God has designed each of us in unique ways. We should be careful that we never compare our children with each other or someone else's kids. We should also avoid comparing them with an image of the perfect child we might have formed in our mind or read about in a book. Comparisons are a poison in a home because they actively undermine the grace-filled environment we want to cultivate. Even unconscious comparisons can eventually seep into the souls of our children. Our children sense when we compare them with others, even if we may not articulate it. We need to remember that God looks at each one of our sons and daughters as unique and wonderful, and so should we. Ask God for his help to do this. Affirm what is unique and special in each of your children. Do this openly, repeatedly, and joyfully. What do you love about your child? Tell him. Let her know. Tell others and let your children overhear you. Shout it, sing it, write it, text it, tweet it, and don't stop. If you worry that your child will get a big head, don't! They are growing up in a world that will do all it can to tear them down. Your calling is to notice and praise each child's God-given gifts, abilities, and bents. This is about more than merely building their self-esteem or being a proud parent. It is an affirmation and celebration of God's matchless creativity revealed in your child.

You will discover that it is easiest to notice the unique strengths and gifts of a child who is most like you. It takes more time and commitment if your son or daughter is quite different than you, and you'll have to look closer. If you are extroverted and your daughter is quiet and reflective, don't push her to be like you or subtly make her feel like she does not measure up. Tell her that you love how she really thinks things through and reflects before she speaks. Praise the child who is quiet and thoughtful as much as you do the child who is social and outgoing.

STUDY, STUDY, AND THEN STUDY SOME MORE

Kevin and I are students of our children. We are serious about knowing them, listening to what they say, and studying what they like and dislike. Our three sons are now in their twenties, and we are still learning new things about each one as they continue growing into adulthood. By watching them and asking questions, we learn how to better encourage them in their faith.

Two of our boys are highly verbal and expressive. The third is very articulate, but he tends to be quiet. While all three of our boys responded to the basic message of the gospel at a very young age, their public declaration of faith in a church setting came at different times in their lives. One of our sons did not feel ready to make a public profession of faith until well into his teenage years. We were patient, prayerful, and did not push him. When he was ready, he took the step, and it was real.

We even discovered that the way we taught our boys to love and read the Bible differed from son to son. We could not come up with a set plan and ask all three to follow it in lock step. We had to raise each one according to his unique bents and God-given wiring. As each one has grown, we have seen him become the man God wants him to be.

SHARE THE GOSPEL

How did we share the message of Jesus with our children? The answer is simple. We did it *repeatedly* and *organically*. We articulated the message of the gospel in countless settings and in many different ways. We did not wait until just the right moment. We told the story often and spoke of God's love and grace in Jesus, whenever it naturally fit into the flow of life.

In one of his books, *Reckless Faith*, Kevin looks at the story Jesus tells in the gospel of Luke about a farmer who scatters his seed at planting time.[7] The farmer is recklessly extravagant with the seed. He throws it on rocky soil, hard soil, shallow soil, and good soil. The farmer spreads seed everywhere, not knowing what kind of soil it will land on. One message of this parable is that we should be liberal and generous with the seed of the good news of Jesus. Our children should hear us talk about the gospel as a normal part of our life together. In each home this will look a little different, but there are some common refrains in every setting.

Your Testimony

Tell your children how you came to faith in Jesus. Share how you came to know the reality of your sin and your need for a Savior. Explain what it means to confess your sin and embrace the forgiveness Jesus offers through his suffering and death on the cross. Let your children know how your life has changed because of the gift of forgiveness you received from Jesus. Do this in simple words that are age appropriate for your children. Share this story over and over, whenever it is appropriate. Tell your story with joy, thankfulness, and wonder.

Dads are fond of recounting great moments in their sports careers. Kids hear these stories countless times, and yet dad always finds a reason to tell them again. Sadly, many dads can go a long time without telling their children how they became a follower of Jesus. It may be thought of as a private moment, but it should not be. Dads and moms should be just as excited and eager to tell their spiritual story as they are to talk about other epic moments in their lives.

Our boys have heard my conversion story many times through the years. On a particular Sunday when I was five years old, I was thinking about what I had learned that morning in Sunday school. I was on the couch in the living room, and my mom was in the kitchen cooking chicken noodle soup. In my heart I prayed, asking Jesus to forgive me and come into my life. I told him I wanted to spend the rest of my life following him. At that moment, I felt a rush of joy that I can still remember forty-six years later. I was born again!

My story is not about bad choices and running away from God in rebellion. That was not my journey. I share with my boys how God worked in my young heart and how that moment of receiving the love and grace of Jesus changed everything for me. From that moment on, I stayed close to Jesus. I love him and know he loves me. My boys have heard me speak of this often.

Kevin's story is quite different from mine. He grew up in a non-Christian home, but during his high school years his sister became a Christian. She began attending a church regularly and invited him to her youth group. He was hostile and resistant at first, even as she tried to love and serve him. He rejected every invitation she extended until a special casino night outreach event finally sparked his interest.[8] When Kevin shares his testimony, he talks about meeting a cute girl at the church, and his interest in her kept him coming back. The following summer, Kevin went on a church-sponsored water skiing trip, where he was a captive audience on a houseboat for a week. By the end of that week he had given his heart to Jesus. Kevin and I have very different conversion stories, and our sons have heard both of them many times. They know that surrendering our lives to Jesus and committing to follow him has made all the difference in the world for both Kevin and me.

Stories of God's Presence and Power

We also shared stories of God's presence and power with our children. Our boys needed to hear how we experienced God's power guiding and filling us, and we often told them about how God was working in our lives. We shared moments when God showed up, amazed us, and revealed his glory to us. In addition, we told stories of God's presence. Jesus told his followers that it was better for them that he would go away because then he would send the Holy Spirit to be with them.[9] The Holy Spirit dwells in the heart and life of every believer. When we walk with Jesus, God reveals his presence in startling and beautiful ways. In times of deep pain and loss, the Spirit draws near. He reveals himself and gives us confidence in moments of fear and insecurity. Through the years we have shared testimony after testimony of how God is with us in joyful times and during deep pain. Even now that they are adults, we still tell our boys stories of God's work in our lives, and we are delighted to hear about the great things God is doing in their lives.[10]

We are thankful that this was a normal part of our conversations with the boys. Start doing this when your children are young, and it will become part of the fabric of your life together.

Sharing the message of Jesus is about more than trying to get your children to profess faith. It is a journey of learning to know each child, praying for them, pointing them toward the Savior, and telling them the gospel story. For us, it meant telling our conversion stories regularly and speaking often about how God was working in our lives. There are natural times for each of our children to respond to Jesus' invitation to be born again.[11] Our part, as parents, is to raise, teach, and love each of our children according to how God has made them. As we do, they will respond when they are ready and in a way that fits them. We believe this leads to a healthy walk with Jesus.

BECOMING A LIGHTHOUSE

Try one of these ideas in your home and with your family . . .

Study Their Style. Watch and study each of your children. Make mental notes or even write down your observations. Learn all you can about what motivates them, how they solve problems, the way they gather information, and their personal learning style. Begin the process of becoming a student of your child.

Celebrate Their Uniqueness. Make a point of telling each of your children, no matter how old they are, one thing about their unique temperament and wiring that you really appreciate and love. In addition, look for an opportunity to affirm in front of your whole family something that is unique about each child. This can be at a meal, driving in the car, or in some other setting when your family is together.

Have Story Time. In the coming week, tell each of your children a story about how you have experienced God's power and presence in a specific situation. Make sure this encounter with God has taken place in the last few months.

Chapter Three

The Timing of the Spirit

Sherry

"The people living in darkness have seen a great light; on those living in the land of the shadow of death a light has dawned." From that time on Jesus began to preach, "Repent, for the kingdom of heaven has come near."

— Matthew 4:16 – 17

When Jesus spoke again to the people, he said, "I am the light of the world. Whoever follows me will never walk in darkness, but will have the light of life."

— John 8:12

It is true that Bible prayers in word and print are short, but the praying men of the Bible were with God through many a sweet and holy wrestling hour. They won by few words but long waiting.

— E. M. Bounds

Parents often ask us **if their child is too young to make a genuine commitment to Jesus**. We tell them it's not a question of age but of the heart. I remember sitting at the kitchen table with our first son, Zach, when he was just four years old. He told me quite clearly that he wanted to ask Jesus to come into his life. I had my own memorable experience of asking Jesus to be Lord of my life at a similar age. Still, I wanted to make sure that he grasped the magnitude of this moment, so I asked the Lord to help me.

I shared my excitement with him, and we talked about the good news of Jesus Christ to make sure that he understood the basics of the gospel. And to check his heart, I told him I would love for him to share his desires with his dad as well. I felt this would be a good sign of his desire to make this commitment. If God was moving in Zach's heart and he genuinely wanted to respond, it would still be in his heart when Kevin came home.

You can imagine how my heart soared when it was the first thing he said when his dad came home from work that night. We sat together at the kitchen table, and our firstborn son invited Jesus into his life. It was genuine. He was not too young. This was the same son who two years later, at the age of six, told us he wanted to be a minister. Today, he is living out that call. Never underestimate the power of God!

MAKING THE INVITATION

When is the right time to invite a son or daughter to receive God's grace and enter a saving relationship with Jesus? There is no exact time or age when all children should receive Jesus. While it is wonderful and valuable to give children a strong Christian education in our homes, schools, and churches, we also need to realize that God calls each person in his timing, and each child grows at their own God-given pace. Some churches have a confirmation process, catechism class, or other formal training process, and these can be a wonderful blessing that helps a child learn the truth and grow in their understanding of the faith. Whatever the process may be, though, it should not demand or require that every child respond to the invitation of the gospel at the same time. We should never try to force children into the same mold or put them on the same timetable when it comes to professing their faith.

Instead, we should pray for our children, get to know them, listen, and be discerning. Some kids come at things head-on and want to take the step of faith early in life. This is a joy! Other children take their time, sort things out, and need room to reflect and process. Pushing them to respond too early can push them away from Jesus. Again, as parents we should study our children and learn how they are wired. This helps us raise each one in a way that fits who God is making them and calling them to be.

We discovered that our son Zach is a conventional learner, very linear and logical. I taught him colors at a young age, and he could repeat them back to me in no time at all. I pointed to the cards with pictures of green things and said, "green." I pointed again, and Zach said, "green." He got it! When our second son was about the same age, I tried the same approach. I got my green cards out, expecting the same response, and when Josh didn't respond, I was concerned.

When Kevin came home and I explained how Josh just didn't seem to grasp the concept of color, Kevin laughed. He said to me, "You are trying to teach him like you taught Zach. But remember, he is not Zach. He is Josh. His learning style is reflective and very self-directed. You need to help him become part of the discovery process." To this day, if you try to get Josh to parrot back something, he will look at you with a wry smile, and chances are, he will not play along.

I remember one incident, in particular, when Josh was about thirteen years old. Kevin bought a new phone system for our home, but he didn't bother reading the instructions or even attempt to set it up. He told me, "When Josh gets home from school he will take care of it." When Josh came home from school that day, Kevin was sitting on the living room floor with all the phones, chargers, and instructions in front of him. Kevin didn't say a word, but he tried to look like he was working hard to figure the system out. Josh sat down next to Kevin and started asking questions. Then he picked up the instructions and began reading. After a few minutes, Josh asked his dad if he could set up the phone system. He read the entire instruction booklet and got to work. Kevin wandered away to do something else.

About an hour later, Josh told us that the whole system was set up. Each phone was programmed and titled for the room it went in. He taught us how the system worked and even set up the voicemail program. This was a clear illustration to me of how Josh learns and makes decisions. Josh is the type of person who would recoil at feeling pushed to believe in Jesus or make a public declaration of faith before he was ready. He has always needed to explore, learn, investigate, and come to his own conclusions in his own time. And there is nothing wrong with this. This is the way he was made. He did not feel pressure to join his brothers when they decided to receive Jesus and join the church. Josh was still learning, listening, and moving toward faith in the Savior. Pressure would have pushed him away, and we knew it. So we gave him the space and time he needed.

As you share the gospel, be prayerful and wise. Don't force it, but always be open and ready. Look for those organic, natural moments that the Holy Spirit provides. Whether you are sharing the gospel with a child, parent, cousin, or sibling, there are some helpful things to keep in mind.

1. LISTEN TO THE HEART

God is at work in your child's heart. Before you named your son or daughter, God was already moving in their life.[1] He loves your child more than you do. God is also at work in the lives and hearts of your extended family members. We are not called to force or manipulate. We are simply to scatter the seed of the gospel and bring the water of God's grace. Only God changes hearts.

We must tune in to the heartbeats of family members. When they are more receptive, we must go deeper. When they are resistant, we must slow down and not force it. Ask for the Holy Spirit to give you wisdom, and don't come with an agenda to unload your opinions or ideas onto a family member. Do your best to discern where their heart is and respond accordingly.

Sharing the message of Jesus with their children is the most important thing parents will ever do. As you study your children and pray for them, be sure to wait on God's timing. You will always be scattering seed, teaching, loving, and pointing them to Jesus. The times you invite them to respond to the gospel are very important. Let them initiate. Listen for times when they are asking big questions. Wait on God's leading.

2. INVITE AND DON'T PRESSURE

It is unwise and unloving to pressure, force, or manipulate your child to make a response to Jesus. Our call is to invite. Even Jesus stands at the door and knocks; he does not kick it down.[2] Some parents push their children to respond to Jesus. They lean hard on their children, getting them to say a prayer, walk the aisle, or raise their hand as soon as possible instead of tenderly leading and inviting.

There is nothing wrong with a child making a response early in life as long as it is from the heart. It should not be to make their parents happy or impress church leaders. Children who go through the motions without a real move of the Holy Spirit in their heart can end up very confused. If they do not have an understanding of the gospel they might not be making an authentic commitment to the Savior.

Some parents use strange stories or motivations to get their child to commit to Christ. Kevin and I were once at a camp where one of the speakers talked about being pressured into receiving Jesus by his big brother. His well-meaning sibling took him to the kitchen stove and said, "Would you like to spend forever in an oven like that?" He said, "No! I would not." Then his big brother told him he needed to receive Jesus right now. What do you think an eight-year-old child will say at a moment like that? Of course he prayed! He went on to tell us that his commitment to Jesus was not real, and he wandered spiritually for several years. Thankfully, he came to understand the love of God, the grace of Jesus, and the truth of the gospel. When he finally understood the message of God's grace and forgiveness he turned to Christ and made an authentic commitment.

Some pastors and parents like to talk about the guy who did not press his friend hard enough to make a decision for Christ. That friend walked away from the conversation and was hit by a truck. The moral of the story: force a response to Jesus as soon as possible or you will live with the guilt of someone else's eternal destiny. Pastors and youth leaders tell variations of this story, and it is always unhelpful. It does two things that are unfair and theologically inappropriate.

First, it places the job of salvation on those who share the message of Jesus. We must remember that *we* don't save anyone. We scatter the seed of the good news and bring spiritual water, but only God can bring life and growth. Placing responsibility in parents' hands for the salvation of their children pushes them to pressure their children to make a decision. But this is unbiblical and unhealthy.

Second, this way of thinking tends to heap guilt on the person sharing the good news. It makes them feel like they are eternally responsible if a person does not make a decision for Jesus. Again, this is based on poor theology and leads to fear and manipulation.

As we interact with both our children and our extended family, we should *invite* them to Jesus. Forcing them is not healthy, organic, or Christlike. We can share the gospel story and ask, "Does this make sense?" We can invite, "Would you like to receive God's grace and become a follower of Jesus?" We can encourage our children and family to take the next step toward the Savior, confessing their sin and putting their faith in him. But we must not force, pressure, or manipulate.

3. A "NO" IS NOT REJECTION

As you live a life of organic outreach in your home and among family members, you will have many opportunities to have spiritual conversations. When you ask a family member, "Would you like to pray and receive God's grace through faith in Jesus?" there is a good chance they will say something like, "I'm just not there yet," or, "I still have some questions," or even, "I am not even close to that point." Don't get discouraged. They are not rejecting you. In many cases they are not even rejecting Jesus. They are still on a journey toward the Savior.

Don't overreact in these times. Keep living your life of faith in natural and joy-filled ways. Keep having conversations. Let your light shine. When someone says they are not ready to take that definitive step of faith, let them know you want to keep the conversation going in the days and weeks ahead. Kevin and I have had dozens of these moments when a family member seemed ready but did not take the step to confess their sin and receive Jesus. Most of these people are now followers of Jesus.

4. REJOICE AND DISCIPLE

The best moments in life are when a child or family member says yes to Jesus. When they confess their sins and accept the amazing grace of Jesus as the payment for their sins, everything changes.[3] They are no longer just members of your earthly family, but they become members of the family of God. This means you will be together forever in heaven. You are now part of an eternal family.

As a children's director for several years, I had many opportunities to share the gospel with the children I taught. Because some of the younger children had a difficult time with the brutality of the cross, I thought carefully about how to handle this subject as I shared the gospel with them, wanting not to minimize the truth of what Jesus suffered while communicating it in a way that they could grasp. Here is an example of how I shared the gospel with them. Hopefully this will be helpful as you think about different ways of sharing the good news of Jesus with your children.

God has given us the gift of Jesus because he loves us so much. Jesus came to the earth and died on the cross for all of us. Maybe you are wondering why Jesus had to die in such an awful way. *We don't live the way God wants us to live.* Sometimes we do bad things, we say things that are not true or nice, and we even think things we know are wrong. *These bad actions, words, and thoughts are called sin.*

Because we are not living the way God wants us to live, and because we all do wrong things, God *must punish our sins. Jesus loves us so much that he offered to take the punishment for us.* It says in the Bible that everyone sins. Every one of us falls short of what God wants for us. You and I have done things, said things, and thought things that God is not happy with. We have even failed to do things that God wanted us to do. Jesus had a lot of punishment to take. That's why he died on the cross in such an awful way. We can be set free because Jesus has done this for us. He has taken our punishment for us. This is forgiveness.

We know this is true because the Bible teaches it very clearly. There is another thing the Bible tells us that we all need to know. Jesus gives his forgiveness only to those who want it. We have to ask Jesus to forgive us and come into our life. *If we come to Jesus and are sorry for those wrong things in our life, he will forgive all of our sins and wash us clean.*

If we know we have sinned, if we are sorry for what we have done, and if we believe Jesus died to take our punishment, we can be certain that Jesus will always forgive our sins.

Jesus loves you so much that he was willing to die on the cross so you would not have to take the punishment for your sins. If you believe this and know Jesus wants to forgive you for your sins, you can be positive that Jesus wants to forgive you and be with you forever. He wants to come into your life so that you will be his friend and one day go to heaven to be with him forever. When you believe that Jesus has done this for you and you are sorry for the wrong things you have done, said, and thought, you are ready to ask Jesus to come into your life. Jesus loves you so much.

However you choose to communicate the message, it's important to make the essentials clear:

1. We don't live the way God wants.
2. Our bad actions, words, and thoughts are called sin.
3. God must punish our sins.
4. Jesus loves us, and he has offered to be punished for our sins.
5. If we come to Jesus and are sorry for the sin in our lives, Jesus forgives us and makes us clean.

Make sure that your children recognize their need for Jesus, understand what he has done for them, dying in their place, and are aware of their need to ask for his forgiveness. Most of all, communicate to your children that God does all of this for them because he loves them very much.

When a child or family member receives the amazing grace of God through faith in Jesus, it is time to stop and throw a party. This is a moment worthy of celebration. Make a point of rejoicing. Have a special dinner. Take a picture. Mark the date on your calendar. It is a big deal. Share the news with other family members who are followers of Jesus and invite them to pray for this new believer. A commitment to Jesus is the beginning of a whole new chapter of life. Now it is time to help this person take the next steps of spiritual growth. It is important for them to learn to read and study the Bible, grow in prayer, use their gifts to serve others, share their faith, and so much more.[4]

BECOMING A LIGHTHOUSE

Try one of these ideas in your home and with your family ...

Heart Check. Spend some time reflecting and praying about each of your children. Where do you sense their heart is with Jesus? How open are they to the gospel? What could be standing in the way of their knowing and walking with Jesus? How can you help each of your children connect more closely with Jesus?

God's Timing. As adults, we can move fast and unknowingly pressure our children to make spiritual commitments they are not ready for. Ask God to help you walk with each of your children at a pace that works for them. If you are very goal oriented and tend to drive yourself hard, be sensitive that you don't do this with your children. Confess to God, and even to your children, if you have been pressuring them. Ask the Holy Spirit to help you spread the seed of the gospel always, give invitations regularly, but never pressure your kids to take a step they are not ready to take.

Next Steps. If you have a son or daughter who has received Jesus as their Savior, be sure you rejoice in this reality often. Do all you can to help each of your children connect with God in ways that fit their style and help them go deeper in faith. If you are not sure where to begin, consider getting a copy of the book *Seismic Shifts* and using it as a tool for family growth in Bible study, prayer, worship, godly relationships, and reaching out to others with the grace of Jesus.

Chapter Four

Reaching Your Extended Family

Kevin

Come, descendants of Jacob, let us walk in the light of the
Lord.

— Isaiah 2:5

The Great Commission is not an option to be considered;
it is a command to be obeyed.

— Hudson Taylor

My wife, Sherry, grew up in a wonderful Christian home, and today all of her siblings are devoted followers of Jesus thanks to years of prayer by her parents. In fact, not only their children but also all of their grandchildren love and believe in Jesus. This brings great joy to Sherry's folks and to the entire extended family, which is filled with committed and passionate followers of Jesus.

My family is very different. It is filled with great people whom I love deeply, but it was never a hotbed of evangelical fervor. I was the rare apple that fell far from the family tree. Yet by God's grace, many of my family members have now made commitments to Jesus and are walking with him. In fact, reaching my extended family with the gospel has been a consuming passion of my life since the day I accepted Jesus as my Savior and Leader. I long each and every day for them to know and love Jesus. I hunger for them to experience his amazing grace and life-changing friendship. I pray for them and seek opportunities to share the good news with them. Over the past three decades, I have learned some valuable lessons about how to reach out to family members and share the grace of Jesus in organic and natural ways.

PATIENCE, PATIENCE, PATIENCE

Most important, I've learned that sharing the love of Jesus with members of your extended family is not a sprint. It is a marathon. Organic outreach to parents, siblings, grandparents, aunts, uncles, and in-laws takes time and Spirit-granted patience. I have one family member who comes from a very intellectual background. He is a deep thinker and a committed reader, and he waffled between atheism and agnosticism. I prayed for him, shared my journey with Jesus, and presented the gospel to him on many occasions over two decades. Sometimes when I was praying the hardest and having some of the best spiritual conversations with him, he seemed farther from God than ever. It just didn't make sense to me. One day he would be open, the next he would be pushing back or pulling away. I knew there were spiritual battles taking place, but it was very frustrating.

I gave him books like *Mere Christianity* by C. S. Lewis, *Evidence That Demands a Verdict* by Josh McDowell, and *The Case for Christ* by Lee Strobel. Though he read the books and reflected on them, he would not take that step of faith to believe in Jesus. As much as I loved this guy, there were times when I felt disheartened, discouraged, and ready to give up. I was tempted numerous times to move on to greener pastures and focus on people who seemed more open to the gospel. But God kept calling me to pray, share yet again, and look for new ways to connect him to Jesus.

After nearly twenty years, his heart began to soften. He started asking new questions about Jesus, the Bible, and the Christian faith with a sense of urgency and openness. Over time he had thought through many of his questions, but he realized he could never make it all the way to Jesus through his intellect. There needed to be a step of faith, a genuine surrender. When he finally cried out to Jesus for cleansing and new life, he was transformed. It was a joy to watch! The Holy Spirit swept in like a fresh spring breeze and brought life to this man. A new kindness marked his interactions with other family members. A gracious spirit took over his heart. His whole life direction shifted toward the things of God.

It took two decades of patient prayer, sharing, friendship, and risk-taking conversations, but it was all worth it. I know that there were times I could easily have given up. And I am so thankful that patience is one of the fruits of the Spirit.[1]

Pray for patience as you reach out to members of your immediate or extended family. Don't give up on them. Even as I write this, I still have family members who are not followers of Jesus. I have been praying for some of them for almost thirty-five years. I've had hundreds of conversations with them, have shared countless stories of how God has moved in my life, and have presented the good news of Jesus on more occasions than I can remember. I grow weary and discouraged at times. In these moments, I do what I hope you will learn to do: I pray for power and patience. Then I press on. I remember that God was patient with me, and I seek to be patient with them, knowing that God works through the prayers of his people in his time.

A LINK IN THE CHAIN

Reaching your extended family is a marathon, requiring endurance and a long-term commitment, but it is also a relay race. Have you ever watched a relay? One member of the team runs as hard as they can, pouring out every ounce of strength and energy, then they strain forward and hand the baton to the next competitor. Each member of the team does their part in the race and then relies on another person for the next leg.

We need to remember that we are part of a team when it comes to sharing the gospel. You don't run alone! One of the first people to impact my faith was my granny. My dad's mother prayed for my siblings and me to know the love of God when we were very young. Later, a committed Christian babysitter named Cheryl impacted my life with her gracious spirit and consistent kindness and by sharing Bible stories. She even took me to church and Sunday school a few times. When she became a follower of Jesus, my sister Gretchen took up the baton, praying for me and inviting me to her youth group. Once I started attending youth group, two college guys named Doug and Glenn befriended me, modeled a joyful Christian life, and told me the story of Jesus. At the same time, Dan Webster, the youth pastor, brought powerful and relevant messages to a big room full of high school kids. His leg of the race came at a time when my heart was growing soft toward God. Finally, Doug Webster and Doug Fields presented the gospel and gave me an opportunity to respond and receive the Savior.

Each one of these people carried the baton for part of the race. They were one more link in the chain God used to reach me and move me toward faith in Jesus. Not all were present when I crossed the line of faith, confessed my sins, and received Jesus as Savior on a houseboat on the Sacramento Delta. Yet each of these people was present in my heart. Every link in that chain mattered. All of them ran their leg of the race and did their part to point me toward the Savior.

When it comes to reaching out to our family members, our prayer should be, "Lord, let me be one link in the chain." Ask God to use your testimonies of faith to touch family members. Seek opportunities to share the simple message of the birth, life, death, and resurrection of Jesus. When the moment is right, invite people in your family to confess their sins, receive Jesus, and begin a new life of faith as a Christian. Your link might be sharing your testimony. God might use you to model joy in the tough times. You might be the one to share the gospel one more time and see the light of the Holy Spirit come alive in a family member's eyes as they pray to receive Jesus and repent of sin. Your call is to do your part, whatever it is. As you walk down the road of faith with family members, pray for God to send many other people to be links in the chain.

When my younger brother was living in Europe and training staff at a new restaurant, I prayed that God would send other people his age to come alongside him and show him the love of Jesus. I believed he needed to hear of God's grace and power from his peers and not just from his big brother. When he began dating a wonderful Christian girl I prayed she would influence him for the gospel. With time he became a follower of Jesus, and they ended up getting married, having a beautiful family, and serving Jesus together as they now minister in their home, the public schools, and a local church. I was part of Jason's story, one link in the chain. I carried the baton for part of the race. God used me, and many other people, in his life. I am eternally grateful that I can be part of God's plan to reach people with the gospel, but I always remember that I am just one of many.

You have a role in the life of every person you know and love who is not yet a follower of Jesus. You have a calling to bring the message of Jesus to these people. As you reach out to them in natural and organic ways, remember that you are not alone. You are part of a God-ordained team of people who run the race together. Pray for the other people on your team and rejoice that you can be one source of influence in the lives of your family members.

FAITH COMES BY HEARING

Pray for your family members who need Jesus. Be patient as you walk with them. Work with others to reach your family members, and rejoice in this Spirit-led partnership. As you do all of this, also be sure to articulate how God is working in your life. Stories of faith have more power than you realize and should not be reserved for immediate family but should be shared with extended family as well. They know us. They remember what we were like before we had faith in Jesus. They saw us transformed by the presence of the Holy Spirit. We need to explain the source of this change, the origin of our joy, and the reason for our hope.[2] We should not be afraid or hesitant to tell stories of God's work in our lives.

Some people say, "I'll be the link in the chain that loves and serves but never says a word." But this is not a biblical option. You need to be able to articulate the life-saving message of the gospel. This should not be a memorized speech. It should be a natural telling of the Jesus story. To help you learn to share this story with others, I've included a version that covers all of the essential elements of the gospel. Familiarize yourself with the story such that you can comfortably retell it in a way that is natural for you. However you choose to communicate the gospel, the important thing is that you are ready to share it with your family members when the time is right.[3]

THE GOSPEL, GOD'S GOOD NEWS

God's love for people is huge and amazing. God loves you more than words can express. The Bible is filled with this message. The starting point of salvation is love. No matter how you feel about yourself and no matter how others treat you, God's love is constant. He longs to be in an intimate relationship with you.

> But you, Lord, are a compassionate and gracious God, slow to anger, abounding in love and faithfulness.
> — *Psalm 86:15*

> See what great love the Father has lavished on us, that we should be called children of God! And that is what we are!
> — *1 John 3:1*

Human beings broke their relationship with God by sinning. *Sin* is the word the Bible uses to describe anything you do that is not consistent with God's plan. Any thought that does not honor God, any word that is unkind, and any action that hurts others or is contrary to God's will is called sin. The Bible also teaches that when we know there is something good we should do and we fail to do it, this also is sin. In light of this definition, it is clear that we all sin quite a bit, every day.

Sin destroys our relationship with God. He still loves us, but our sin drives a wedge between him and us. God wants a restored relationship, but because God is perfectly pure (holy), he can't just look the other way and pretend we have not sinned. Because he is perfectly fair (just), he must punish sin. The Bible makes it clear that there is only one punishment for sin: the death penalty. It might sound harsh, but God's absolute holiness and unparalleled justice demand that this ultimate punishment be paid.

This is the worst news imaginable. Because of our sin, we are all separated from the God who loves us. We are condemned to death because of our sin. This bad news can seem overwhelming until we realize what God did to restore our relationship with him and free us from the death sentence that hangs over us.

> All have sinned and fall short of the glory of God.
>
> —*Romans 3:23*

> For the wages of sin is death, but the gift of God is eternal life in Christ Jesus our Lord.
>
> —*Romans 6:23*

God did something about this problem, and what he did is the greatest news ever. God offers to pay the price for us. He came to this earth as a man, Jesus. This is what we celebrate on Christmas. Jesus was God in a human body. Jesus lived a real life, with real joys, pain, and temptations, and he experienced everything we face. But here is the difference: Jesus never sinned. He did not have one thought, motive, or action that dishonored his Father. He never spoke a word that was hurtful or wrong.

Jesus was accused of crimes he did not commit and was condemned to death. He was stripped, beaten, mocked, and nailed to a cross, executed as a common criminal. Jesus suffered this brutal death so that we would not have to pay the price for our sins. His death, the death we deserve to die, was the payment. Then he rose from the grave in glory as a sign of his victory over sin and death. If we accept Jesus, we enter a relationship with God the Father, and instead of death we are given eternal life.

The gospel is called the good news because we are offered a pardon for all of the wrongs we have ever done and ever will do. We can have new life and a restored relationship with God through Jesus. We don't earn it or deserve it, and we can't take credit for it. All we can do is accept it.

> For God so loved the world that he gave his one and only Son, that whoever believes in him shall not perish but have eternal life.
>
> —*John 3:16*

> This is love: not that we loved God, but that he loved us and sent his Son as an atoning sacrifice for our sins.
>
> —*1 John 4:10*

How can a person accept Jesus, have their sins washed away, and enter a restored relationship with God? Salvation is a gift; it is not earned by checking the boxes on some to do list of good works. Salvation can be received only through faith in Jesus. Faith begins by asking Jesus to forgive you and become the leader of your life. This step of faith means admitting you have sinned against God and are sorry for your sins. It means asking God to help you live a new and changed life that honors him.

You don't have to know a lot of fancy religious terms. Tell God that you know you have sinned. Express your sorrow for your sin and ask for the forgiveness that comes through the price Jesus paid when he died on the cross. Invite Jesus to enter your life and lead you from this moment on, all the way into eternity. You can express this prayer in your own words, or you can use a simple prayer like this one:

> Dear God, I am coming to you to express that I need you more than I have ever known and to confess my sins. I have thought things, said things, and done things that do not please you. I realize my sins cause me to be under a death sentence. I know you sent Jesus, your only Son, to pay the price for my sins by dying in my place on the cross. I believe that Jesus is alive, risen from the dead, and with me right now. Jesus, thank you for paying the price for me. I need your forgiveness. I want you to enter my life and become my leader from this moment on. Thank you for all you have done and all you will do in my life. Amen!

When you have lifted up this prayer from a sincere heart you can be confident that you are now in a restored relationship with God and all of your sins are forgiven.

> If we confess our sins, he is faithful and just and will forgive us our sins and purify us from all unrighteousness.
>
> —1 John 1:9

> As far as the east is from the west, so far has he removed our transgressions from us.
>
> —Psalm 103:12

> If you declare with your mouth, "Jesus is Lord," and believe in your heart that God raised him from the dead, you will be saved.
>
> —Romans 10:9

WHAT IS THE GOSPEL?

We live in an age when many church-attending Christians are confused about the gospel. What is the gospel? The word *gospel* means "good news." The gospel is news before it is anything else — it is the announcement of what God has done for us in Jesus Christ. By God's grace and through the power of the Holy Spirit, the announcement of this news brings change and transformation. But we need to remember that this change is not the gospel; it is the fruit of the gospel.

Bringing clean water to people in need is not the gospel. Providing food and clothing for the poor is not the gospel. Kind acts of service in various shapes and forms are not the gospel. All of these acts of compassion are important, and Jesus calls us to engage in them. But these actions in and of themselves are not the gospel. They are the fruit that grows in our lives when we have embraced the good news of Jesus. The gospel is the simple message of Jesus' life, death, and resurrection for the sake of our sins. This message, communicated with words, has always been the gospel. And it will always be the gospel.

Our acts of mercy and compassion can be thought of as *pre*-evangelism, opening the way for the gospel. But our acts of service, no matter how compassionate and lovingly motivated, are never enough to save people. People need to hear the story of Jesus and the message of God's love revealed in Christ's life, death, and resurrection. The gospel is the life-changing message of the salvation found in Jesus alone. The truth of the gospel and the grace of Jesus are what transforms us.

The message we are called to communicate is the same one the apostle Paul spoke with such clarity and conviction two thousand years ago: "Now, brothers and sisters, I want to remind you of the gospel I preached to you, which you received and on which you have taken your stand. By this gospel you are saved, if you hold firmly to the word I preached to you. Otherwise, you have believed in vain. For what I received I passed on to you as of first importance: that Christ died for our sins according to the Scriptures, that he was buried, that he was raised on the third day according to the Scriptures."[4]

Our actions may give someone evidence that God is at work, that he loves them and cares for them, but our actions can't bring the hope of eternity. Only the gospel can do that. Our service reveals the presence of Jesus. He is the one who washed the feet of sinful people and shared his life so they could enter a friendship with him that would lead to their salvation. Our compassion and merciful ministry in the world prepare a place for the gospel to be proclaimed, but it still needs to be proclaimed. The Bible teaches that faith comes by hearing the word of God.[5] As people hear the message of the gospel, they are raised to new life through the work of God's Spirit.

DIFFERENT STROKES

This means we need to know the core message of the good news of Jesus, but it doesn't mean that there is only one way to share that message with family members. Though we might share similar DNA and a common family history, each person is unique, so we can't just memorize a script and regurgitate it every time an opportunity presents itself. We don't do this in any other area of life, so why would we do it with the gospel?

Don't expect a one-size-fits-all approach to work as you reach out to your family members. There are truly different strokes for different folks. We need to know how to share the good news of Jesus in a variety of ways so that we can find the way that is most natural for the person we are sharing with. This is the heart of organic outreach: sharing our faith naturally with others. Real evangelism is more than rattling off a memorized message. It is looking a person in the eyes and thinking about who they are. It is knowing their heart and story enough to present the gospel in a way that fits them right where they are. The key is knowing the heart, needs, and spiritual condition of the person to whom you are talking.[6]

I was speaking to a woman in my family who had been investigating the Christian faith in an off-and-on sort of way for about twenty-five years. This particular family member has a passion for music. Music touches her soul in a way that is deep and true to who she is, so over the years I gave her great Christian music. She loved it. The message of Jesus came alive in her heart through that music. Eventually she began attending a wonderful church near her home, and she joined the choir. She was not yet a follower of Jesus, but she loved singing and connecting with the other choir members, and they lovingly welcomed her.

The music helped her come close to God, but she still needed to hear the gospel and be invited to respond. One day, while she and I were sitting in her car in a parking lot, I shared the story of Jesus with her once more. This time she was ready to hear it, and I prayed with her to receive Jesus as she confessed her sins and her need of Jesus' grace. I had the privilege of baptizing her soon afterward. The whole church choir came outside to the church courtyard and sang as she was baptized. What a day of rejoicing!

My approach with each family member is different. I gave books to an intellectual young man in my family. I prayed with a woman in my family who was resistant to the gospel but very open to having me pray for her when she was facing hard times. In each case, however, I still needed to articulate and communicate the content of the gospel in a way they could understand.

As you seek to reach your family with the gospel in natural ways, don't get locked in to some formula. Don't feel like you have to present the gospel in a packaged version you may have been taught. Don't force everyone into the same mold. Instead, get to know each person and discover their passions, dreams, likes, and interests. Meet them where they are as you walk with them toward Jesus.

Jesus showed this approach in his ministry. He met the woman at the well in the desert of her need and brought her the living water of his grace.[7] He met Nicodemus, a religious leader, at night and brought him into the light.[8] Jesus found a tax collector named Zacchaeus in a tree and invited him to spend the rest of his life giving away all he had wrongfully taken from others.[9] Jesus encountered lepers, religious leaders, prostitutes, and fishermen right where they were. He spoke their language. He entered their world. He extended grace long before they asked for it.[10]

TAKING RISKS

There is little risk involved when we share our faith with strangers on a plane or the subway. Chances are we will never see these people again. Sharing the good news of Jesus with a member of our family, however, is risky. Chances are we will be having Thanksgiving supper, Christmas lunch, and family reunions with them for the rest of our lives. You might say, "When I think of sharing the message of Jesus I get really nervous." If you do, pray a lot! Don't let your nerves get the best of you. You love the people in your family. You want them to know the joyful friendship and hope that comes through receiving Jesus.

Take a risk. Love, serve, care, tell your stories of faith, and share the good news of Jesus. But do it naturally—organically. Be bold and gentle. If you come to a moment when it seems appropriate to tell the story of Jesus, simply ask permission. Look at your mom, brother, aunt, or nephew and say, "Would it be okay if I told you about what Jesus did for me and how my relationship with Jesus has transformed my life?" If they say yes, you have permission. Share with ordinary language and sincere excitement. This could be the day your family member becomes your brother or sister in faith as part of God's forever family. If they say, "No thanks, I'm not interested right now," you have learned more about where they are in their spiritual journey. It is always worth the risk!

I wish I could say that every member of my family is now a follower of Jesus, but not all of them are. However, many of them have come to know his love and grace. My older sister, Gretchen, was the first to bow on her knees to Jesus. She has a deep and authentic love for Jesus and has been leading a children's Bible class with the help of her son at a great church in Irvine for many years. My little sister, Lisa, became a follower of Jesus at a young age. She and her husband, Brian, are raising their children to love Jesus. Her company helps people move toward employment, and they do it with a clear Christian worldview.[11] My brother, Jason, loves God with a passion. He and his wife, Mindy, are also teaching each of their kids to love and walk with Jesus. He is serving in a local church as a part-time music director, in addition to his full-time job. Finally, my oldest sister, Ali, committed her life to Jesus, and I baptized her at the church she attended when she gave her heart to the Lord.

My granny, who went to be with Jesus almost two decades ago, prayed for God's hand to move through our family. It has, and it still is! She was a link in the chain, as am I and as is my wife, Sherry. Now our sons are also part of our ministry to the family, along with my siblings and some cousins. In my extended family, there are now many people who are followers of Jesus, but there are still many who have not yet responded to the gospel.

As you minister to your immediate and extended family, be bold and courageous. Be gentle and humble. Ask God for patience. This journey is more like a marathon than a sprint. Remember that you are one important link in the chain, but it is not all up to you. There are few things more glorious than seeing a family member confess faith in Jesus, repent of their sins, and be born again. All heaven rejoices, and so can you.[12] I pray that every member of your family will become a passionate Christian and servant of Jesus. Please pray the same for mine.

BECOMING A
LIGHTHOUSE

Try one of these ideas in your home and with your family ...

Practice Patience. Think about family members who are still far from Jesus. You may have been praying for them and reaching out for years or even decades. If you have grown weary, ask God to grant you patience for the long haul. Commit to continue reaching out, praying, loving, and sharing the message of Jesus with these family members no matter how long it takes.

Pray for Partners. Spend time in prayer thanking God for the other Christians he has sent into the lives of your family members. Give God praise that you are part of a team of people seeking to reach your family. If you have children or extended family members who have very few connections with committed followers of Jesus, ask God to send some new friends, work colleagues, or neighbors who will shine the light of Jesus into their lives.

Speak Good News. Each of our family members is unique and needs to hear the message of Jesus in a way that connects for them. Ask God to give you wisdom to know how to communicate with boldness when the moment comes. As a family, take time to tell each other the story of the gospel. Practice talking through the core message of the gospel: God's love, our sin, Jesus' sacrifice that pays the price for each of us, and the power of the resurrection. Use the examples in this chapter, but don't try to memorize them. Get the core message and put it in your own words. You will shape how you tell the story of Jesus a bit differently for each person you talk with.

Part Two

RAISING CHILDREN OF LIGHT IN A DARK WORLD

The journey is only beginning once our children know and love Jesus. God wants our sons and daughters to join us in shining the light of his love and grace to others. Our children live every day in a world that will throw cold water on their enthusiasm and try to extinguish the flame of God's Spirit that is alive within them. As parents, we have the privilege of raising our children in a way that empowers them to shine.

This happens as we provide a place where our children learn to walk in the light and resist the darkness. Homes of light offer our children a safe haven from the storms of life. They are an emergency room where broken hearts are healed, wounds are bound, and healthy living is taught. Lighthouse homes are places where fun, joy, and play are normative and where our children and their friends love to spend time. Our children learn to shine the light of Jesus when prayer is central in our homes.

The best place for our children to be filled with passion for the gospel and learn to share it with others is right where they live. As parents, we can make our homes places of grace and help our children become bearers of God's light in this dark world.

Chapter Five

The Home as a Safe Haven

Sherry

The LORD is my light and my salvation—whom shall I fear?
The LORD is the stronghold of my life—of whom shall I be
afraid?

—Psalm 27:1

But you, brothers and sisters, are not in darkness so that
this day should surprise you like a thief. You are all children of the light and children of the day. We do not be-
long to the night or to the darkness. So then, let us not
be like others, who are asleep, but let us be awake and
sober.

—1 Thessalonians 5:4 - 6

Sailors understand the value of a safe haven. After time on the
open sea, it feels wonderful to pull in to a harbor to rest, stock up
on supplies, and get ready to head out again. When a storm is brewing,
it is comforting to pull in to a port where there is protection from the
waves and the jagged rocks along the shore. Ships were made for the

open sea, but sailors know that they need safe havens on the way to their destination.

Our homes should be places of safety, havens for our children in this storm-torn world. They should know that their home is a place where they can feel safe, stock up on the supplies they need, and be refreshed to head out for the next adventure. Our children will be able to weather the storms of life if they know they have a safe haven they can sail into.

GOD IS OUR REFUGE

God knows our need for protection and places of safety. The Bible speaks often about God providing a safe place for his people to find refuge from danger and from their enemies' attacks. Read these passages slowly and reflect on how God is presented as a place of safety, shelter, and provision:

> One thing I ask from the LORD,
>   this only do I seek:
> that I may dwell in the house of the LORD
>   all the days of my life,
> to gaze on the beauty of the LORD
>   and to seek him in his temple.
> For in the day of trouble
>   he will keep me safe in his dwelling;
> he will hide me in the shelter of his sacred tent
>   and set me high upon a rock.
> I remain confident of this:
>   I will see the goodness of the LORD
>   in the land of the living.
>
> —Psalm 27:4–5, 13

> For you have been my refuge,
>   a strong tower against the foe.
> I long to dwell in your tent forever
>   and take refuge in the shelter of your wings.
>
> —Psalm 61:3–4

The LORD is my shepherd, I lack nothing.
He makes me lie down in green pastures,
he leads me beside quiet waters,
he refreshes my soul.

—Psalm 23:1–3

The Twenty-third Psalm is often called "The Shepherd's Psalm." Even people who do not consider themselves Christians love the words of this portion of the Bible. Why? Because it is a hope-filled declaration that there is a place where needs are met, where the water is calm and the pastures are green, and where souls can be refreshed. It's a promise that we will find clear direction, that evil does not rule, comfort is offered, and God is near. We all long for such a place. And the good news is that such a place does exist when we are close to the Good Shepherd. As these passages indicate, God himself is our strong tower, our refuge, our fortress, and the only safe haven that will truly bring peace and comfort to a storm-torn life. Ultimately, God is where we find our security and strength. He leads us to quiet waters and provides green pastures. If God dwells in our home and Jesus is alive in us, our children will find a safe haven every time they walk in the door. It doesn't matter if they are seven or twenty-seven; they will feel the peace, warmth, and grace of Jesus when they enter. People will be drawn to the light and warmth our homes emit through our relationships with one another and the evident peace and joy we have from our relationship with God. A safe home is more than a place of physical security—it is a haven because God dwells there and his presence is known.

Many homes are places of turmoil and pain, more like a war zone than a refuge. Many children have no place where they feel secure, not even their own house. There is a desperate need for homes in every community where people feel welcomed and loved. This welcome can be expressed in simple ways: offering words of kindness, greeting each person by name and with a smile, or drawing people into conversations, asking them questions and showing interest in their lives. But before we can do any of this, we need to establish a few foundational practices, boundaries that help us effectively serve the people who enter our home.

FIRST THINGS FIRST

I held my newborn son close to me, firmly in my arms. I was on a plane, preparing for departure, and though I had flown many times before, this felt altogether different. It was my first time experiencing air travel as a new mom. The flight attendant was giving the usual predeparture instructions: "In the event of an emergency, oxygen masks will drop from above your seats. To start the flow of oxygen, pull the mask firmly toward you to extend the plastic tubing. Place the mask over your nose and mouth, slip the elastic band over your head, and tighten the straps as necessary. Although the bag does not inflate, oxygen will flow to the mask. Secure your mask before helping your children or others."

Though I had heard these instructions countless times, that last line caught my attention. "Secure your mask before helping your children or others." I had never noticed it before. I began thinking how selfish that seemed. "You have got to be kidding! If there is an emergency, the first person getting a mask is my baby, not me. What parent would save themselves at the expense of their child?" It didn't take long, however, for me to see the wisdom in her instructions. I realized that if I was going to be of any help to my child, I needed to be alive. If I did not get oxygen, I would pass out and would not be able to help my son. It made perfect sense.

I share this story because I believe it's wise to talk about the things we need to have in place *before* we care for the needs of others. Our homes cannot be places of help and safety for others if we don't have foundations. As we have already said, the most important foundation is that God is an active part of our life. When Jesus rules as Lord, the Holy Spirit is present, and the love of the Father is plain to see, then we can take additional steps to make our home a safe haven.

CONTINUITY

Establishing continuity between our words and actions is the first element of building a home that is a safe haven. Parents who live in a way that is contrary to what they teach create an unstable environment. A disconnect between what a parent says and does cultivates distrust, and it does not make a child feel safe. We asked our oldest son, Zach, to share his thoughts on the importance of continuity between what a parent says and what a parent does.

DO AS I SAY, NOT AS I DO
Zach Harney

In every relationship, there exists a student and a teacher. Though most relationships aren't necessarily framed this way, this is always true. Between two friends, the roles may switch, depending on where each person is in their spiritual journey. The dynamics between a child and a parent are different, however. Though a parent never signs up for the role of teacher that is exactly what they are. From the time the child is born until they leave the house, the parents are the primary instructors and models of Christian morals and values. A child's school teacher, youth group leader, and even pastor can get away with preaching or teaching one thing and living out another, but never a parent. Children are much more perceptive than most people think, and while most parents know this, it is not what their actions imply.

This phrase "Do as I say, not as I do" is born out of lazy and ignorant parenting. It can be heard from the father who lights up a cigarette in front of his child, yet who desperately wants his child to be free of the same vice. It is heard from the mother pouring her final glass of wine for the night, the one that will put her over the edge, past the point of responsibility. It is heard anywhere that a parent wants to escape their parental duties for just a moment, or maybe longer, and their personal desires win over selflessness. This phrase is the get-out-of-jail-free card for parental accountability. The problem is, it doesn't work.

On this earth, a child's most constant example of how to live is their parents. Even a parent who is not present is a model of parenting, and sometimes this model is the most piercing and long-lasting. Children hear what their parents say and see most of what they do. For better or for worse, the home is a place of brutal honesty, where walls are removed and the most instinctual reactions are commonplace. If a Christian parent's goal is to raise sons and daughters that live successful and fruitful lives, then they have to model this; there is no way of getting around it. If a Christian parent teaches Christian values and morality, but does not live it out, their kids will be affected in one way or another. At best, they will subconsciously see their parent as a fraud and someone with little integrity, and at worst, they may turn away from the Christian faith due to the level of hypocrisy that permeates their entire upbringing. When you are a parent, your kids are watching.

I grew up in a home where what was preached was practiced. People often ask me what it was like growing up in a pastor's home, and I tell them that it is the main reason I am the man I am today. Unfortunately, many pastors' kids grow up hearing their fathers or mothers talk about Christian living in church and then see them display very little of what they are constantly teaching. There is one main reason that my favorite pastor is my father, and that is because I know unequivocally that almost every word he preaches from the pulpit is a truth he is either living out currently or working extremely hard at living out on a daily basis. When my mother and father do seminars on how to have a good marriage, it holds weight, because I get to see them every day live out what they are teaching. I have seen countless parents that live out their faith organically in front of their kids, and plenty that don't. Let me tell you, it makes a difference.

You might say, "Well, what about this family who raised their kids right and they still ended up going down the wrong path?" To this I would say that we live in a fallen world in which people have the choice to make the decisions they will, despite what they have been taught. However, this can't be used as an excuse to not put everything into being a Christian example for the younger generation of Christians being raised up, especially if they are your flesh and blood. Christ calls us to be salt and light in a rotting and dark world. He calls us to preserve and give hope, not just for our children but also for all who are lost. The truth of the matter is that the desire to be a Christlike example should not come from wanting to be perceived as a good example by our children but simply from a desire to follow and become more like Christ. When this is someone's sole focus, it will not go unnoticed, but will spill over into every area of their lives, and most importantly to their children.

Continuity does not equal perfection. Parents who seek to be consistent with their children are not guaranteed that all will go well and things will turn out as they hope and pray. But continuity provides a healthy environment where children can feel safe and have a better chance of becoming the kind of people who can shine the light of Jesus in the world around them.

I am grateful for Zach's assessment of us as parents. I am also profoundly aware that if he scoured his memory bank he could recall a fair share of moments when we did not exhibit the kind of continuity we strove to live with. With all of our efforts there were still plenty of times Kevin and I did not behave or react in a Christlike manner. There were plenty of frustrations raising three active boys. On many occasions both Kevin and I had to apologize to each other and our boys when we did not have the strength, the wisdom, or even the desire to make our home the place it needed to be.

Through all of this, God's grace was enough. Even though we often fell short, all three of our boys have memories of a home with consistent love and continuity between what we said and how we lived our lives. For this, we are truly grateful.

ROCK SOLID BELIEFS

A few years ago, my husband had the opportunity to interview Thom Rainer. Thom serves as the president and CEO of LifeWay Christian Resources. He is also the founding dean of the Billy Graham School of Missions and Evangelism and headed up the Rainer Group, a consulting firm that helps churches with health and growth, for more than fifteen years. He has a wealth of insight about evangelism and our culture, having studied both extensively.

In preparation for the interview, Kevin read four of Thom's books; in one of them, *Surprising Insights from the Unchurched and Proven Ways to Reach Them*, Thom shares the results of some surveys he conducted, which show that doctrine matters more to unchurched people than most of us realize.[1] Thom found that Christians who know what they believe and who have strong convictions bring hope in a world where relativism rules. Thom's research showed that most people aren't turned off by doctrines and strong beliefs—they simply want to know if those who follow Jesus actually believe what they say they believe.

Having biblical beliefs and standing strong on our convictions brings stability to a home. We don't have to be legalistic or obnoxiously dogmatic about everything we believe. Rather, we must understand the core of our faith, hold to the fundamentals, and do all of this with humble conviction. Our children, their friends, and anyone who comes into our home should find people who not only know what they believe but are also actively building their lives on that rock-solid foundation.

A few weeks into his first theology class at Bible college, our youngest son called us with an interesting question: "Why didn't you teach me theology when I was growing up?" He observed that many of his fellow students were pretty familiar with the terms being used in his class. He knew we both had theology degrees from seminary and was curious why it seemed absent in our home. We assured him that he understood the doctrines he was learning and had many of the same core beliefs, but we had simply chosen not to use the formal theological terms.

We pointed out different ways in which we had taught him biblical doctrine as he was growing up and helped him see that we had, in fact, quite intentionally integrated biblical theology into his life on a daily basis. But we didn't do this through formal study or reading theology books together. We did it organically, in a way that made it seem like it was just part of life. We didn't make a big deal about it. A few months later our son called us again and thanked us for all the theology he had learned growing up.

A home becomes a safe haven when we teach our children what the Bible says and show them its importance for life. We help them learn to read the Word and come to personal conclusions about what the Scriptures teach. We teach them to ask questions and look to the Bible for answers. We give examples of how the Bible can inform our choices, shape our attitudes, and give guidance as we seek life direction. In a world where so many people have nothing they believe with conviction, we need to show our children that our lives are built on the bedrock of the Bible.

LOVING DISCIPLINE

A home also becomes a safe haven as we show loving, consistent discipline. Parents who care about their children should have well-defined boundaries for them. I remember one of my education professors in college saying, "You must be insistent, persistent, and consistent when you discipline." We sought to live out all three of these in our home.

If there is no discipline in a home, it is not a safe place for a child and can, in fact, become very dangerous for them. Years ago, when our sons were still very young, Kevin coached them in a community soccer league. Once our boys played in a game that got out of control. Kevin was concerned because one of the boys on the other team was using profanity on the field and was being way too physical with our players. In particular, this boy targeted a younger boy on our team who was smaller than the rest of the players. At one point in the game, this older boy shoved our smallest player to the ground and started screaming at him. All of the children stopped playing, scared by what was happening.

Kevin sought to intervene, telling the referee to take charge of the game. A soccer player who is being too rough can be given a yellow card as a warning or, if the behavior merits, can be expelled from the game with a red card. These cards are a form of discipline that helps to keep a game from spinning out of control and becoming dangerous. Kevin suggested that the referee give the player a yellow or red card. Surprisingly, the referee made it clear that he didn't see the need to intervene. "I don't give yellow cards, and I don't give red cards," he said. "I just let the kids play!" After hearing this, Kevin turned to me and said, "This is bad. This could become a real mess." Kevin had played soccer for years, and he knew from experience how quickly things can go bad when there are no boundaries or discipline on the field. When the kids on the other team realized that there would be no consequences for overly physical play, they began playing rougher. And not surprisingly, within a matter of minutes a boy was on the ground with a serious injury. After the injury, Kevin pulled his team off the field and refused to let them play anymore. In his ten years of coaching, I had never seen Kevin pull a team off the field before. But in this case he knew that the lack of discipline would only lead to further injuries and problems. It was an unsafe environment.

Consistent, loving discipline is a gift, whether in a home or on a soccer field. Well-defined boundaries provide safety and security for children, and parents who offer this make their home a safe haven. The Bible speaks about the value of discipline. In Hebrews 12:7 – 11, we learn that God's discipline is one of the signs that we are his beloved children. As the writer indicates, being disciplined is never pleasant, but it trains and prepares a child for godly living: "Endure hardship as discipline; God is treating you as his children. For what children are not disciplined by their father? If you are not disciplined — and everyone undergoes discipline — then you are not legitimate, not true sons and daughters at all. Moreover, we have all had human fathers who disciplined us and we respected them for it. How much more should we submit to the Father of spirits and live! They disciplined us for a little while as they thought best; but God disciplines us for our good, in order that we may share in his holiness. No discipline seems pleasant at the time, but painful. Later on, however, it produces a harvest of righteousness and peace for those who have been trained by it."

Biblical discipline springs from love and leads to maturity, health, and wholeness. Punishment, however, is different. We punish people to uphold justice, inflicting pain upon someone for wrong, unlawful behavior. To communicate the gracious love of God revealed to us in the gospel, we need to make sure that when we correct behavior, we do so as an act of loving discipline and not merely to punish in anger. Practically, this means that we discipline in a way that honors God and communicates love to our children.

1. Affirm and Reinforce Positive Behavior

Whenever you see your child doing something right, give verbal affirmation. Positive words of blessing go a long way. Look for the good they have done and point it out, both in private and when others are around. This was a big priority in our home. You can say things like, "I like the way you are including your younger brother when you have your friends over." Or, "Thank you for making your bed this morning; I think it is great that you do that without being reminded every morning." We tried to focus on the positive things we saw in our children. Again, it takes work to pay attention and notice what they are saying and doing, but it is certainly worth it.

2. Be Clear about Rules and Expectations

Your children should know and understand household rules. Make sure they know the details of the rules and the specific consequences if one is broken. Kevin sometimes wrote out *very* specific rules and posted them where the boys could see them. This wasn't an attempt to be legalistic; it was simply important that we were clear in our expectations. We both agree that it made a significant difference in our home.

I remember when one of our sons, who had been conversing with some elementary school friends, was surprised to learn that they did *not* have regular family meetings to discuss goals, schedules, and guidelines. He also discovered that other parents (the dads in particular) did not provide their kids with written instructions and bullet lists of expectations for household behavior. He had assumed that these were normal behaviors for families and was surprised to find out that they were somewhat unique to our home.

Our homes feel like a safe haven when we communicate well and our children know the rules. We have a friend, Dan Seaborn, who leads a wonderful ministry called Winning At Home. He helps couples build strong and biblical marriages, and he also helps parents build a healthy home for their children.[2] Dan often talks about the importance of having clear household and family rules. In his home there were basically five simple and clear rules:

1. Only positive attitudes allowed.
2. Respect yourself and others.
3. Attend church.
4. Abide by the morals we establish.
5. Use put ups (the opposite of put downs).

In a world where storms rage, clear expectations and household rules build a home that feels safe and solid.

3. Give Warnings and Follow Through

Kids are kids. Even the best-behaved children will have their tough days. If you want to discipline with grace and love, you need to learn to give gentle but firm warnings. You simply say, "If you continue to do that behavior, the consequence will be …" Then you give an appropriate consequence. And you need to follow through. If you say to a child, "This is your final warning," it had better be your last warning. Consistency is essential.

Once one of our sons crossed a clear line, broke a family rule, and received a time of restriction. We gave him an exact number of days he would be confined to our house and let him know he would be doing housework and yard work when he got home from school every day of his restriction. By day two he was trying to negotiate fewer days of restriction and less yard work.

We realized that he believed he could wear us down. It struck us that there had been times we had not followed through with the discipline we started. We got tired, lazy, or just forgot what we had said. When the lights went on we realized our inconsistency was hurting our child. We committed ourselves to being realistic about our warnings and specific discipline we gave our children. But once we told them what we were going to do, we did all we could to work as a team and follow through, even when it was hard for us. This was a great lesson to learn.

4. Make Discipline Be Felt

For discipline to be helpful and productive, it must significantly touch an area that matters to the child—it must be *felt*. Some parents default to sending their son or daughter to their room for the evening. But while they are confined to their room kids can watch TV, go online, communicate on Facebook or Twitter, video chat with their friends, and use their phone. Being confined to their room might not be all that different from most other evenings. A wise and creative parent will learn to identify discipline that actually gets a child's attention. For one teenager, an appropriate consequence might be the loss of phone, computer, or social network use. For another it might involve doing chores around the house. It's important to remember that the point of the discipline is not to humiliate or hurt a child but to redirect their behavior, point them to examine their heart and their motives, and eventually heal. As your children grow up, various kinds of discipline will be required in different seasons of their lives. A loving parent tries to make sure discipline actually has an impact and leads to the desired outcome.

Once, when one of our boys was still very young, he went to the store on his bike without permission. He knew the rules, and when he was caught, the question was not, "Will I be disciplined?" but, "What will Dad and Mom do?" In this case we put him on restriction in our house and yard, and then we added a bonus item. We had him write a list of the reasons why he should not go to Kmart without permission. As we read through his list, we noticed that he started out with some very thoughtful and serious answers, showing us that he understood the danger of going so far from home without permission. We loved that he bolded the first two, letting us know that he understood what we were trying to teach him. And we loved that he brought some humor into the experience. I enjoyed it so much, I kept the list:

Reasons I Should Not Go to the Store without Permission

1. **Get hit by a car**
2. **You don't know where I am**
3. Might be too late
4. We might be going somewhere
5. Might get hurt
6. Parents will get mad at me
7. Parents might give me money
8. Parents might want me to get something
9. Parents want to know where I am
10. Might be too early
11. Might have company coming over
12. Someone might try to kidnap me
13. We might be eating lunch
14. We might be eating dinner
15. You might have a surprise for me (a new deck for my skateboard perhaps)

5. Stay Calm

As you seek to lovingly discipline your children, it's important that you keep a sense of humor and remember that lasting change won't be motivated by their fear of consequences but by respect and love for you and, ultimately, for God. With this in mind, we advise parents who are facing challenging discipline issues with their children to stay calm. As intense as things can get with our children, parents should always keep their cool and never lash out in anger. Whether it's a wild, disobedient two-year-old or a high school student who knows how to push your buttons, disciplining a child can be really frustrating sometimes. Keep the high ground and make sure you stay calm in the midst of conflicts and discipline.

Be committed to showing love, tenderness, and care for your child. Never block them out or give them the silent treatment. This will create insecurity and fear. Your child needs to know that you love them and always will, but you won't allow certain behaviors in your home or family. Kevin remembers how his dad would say, in a firm and booming voice, "That is not acceptable behavior in this household!" Then his dad would sit him down and explain why he was being disciplined. He would do it with kindness, but his discipline was firm. Kevin always knew that his dad loved him and that the discipline he received was designed to make him a better person. Kevin's dad did not call his children names or humiliate them. He made it clear what was not allowed and followed through with consistent and caring discipline when the kids crossed the line.

I had heard Kevin talk about his dad's discipline many times. Then one day, I heard his dad's famous line for myself. One of our boys was behaving in a way that everyone in our home knew was not allowed. With a firm, strong voice Kevin said, "That is not acceptable behavior in this household!"

He explained to our son what consequences he would face, and then he followed through. Set the rules and stick to them. Be fair and loving. Be firm and follow through with what you say. Above all else, make sure God is central in your home and that he is your refuge. Let him be the rock that your whole family lives on.

BECOMING A LIGHTHOUSE

Try one of these ideas in your home and with your family . . .

Continuity Check. As parents we create a safe haven when our words and lives are consistent. There needs to be continuity between what we teach our children and how we live on a daily basis. Examine your life and words. Are there places where you are saying one thing and doing another? If you dare, ask your children if they notice any area in your life where you lack continuity. If you find an inconsistency, adjust your actions to match what you teach your children.

Loving Discipline. Children actually desire for their parents to extend consistent and loving discipline. Give yourself a score on each of the statements below using this simple scale:

1. This is never true of me.
2. This is sometimes true of me.
3. This is consistently true of me.

____ When I see good and positive behavior in my children, I make a point of telling them.

____ I express household rules clearly and reinforce them often.

____ I give appropriate warnings and follow through on discipline with my kids.

____ When I discipline I choose consequences that will impact each child specifically.

____ As I discipline I am calm and don't get overly emotional.

____ I am kind and keep communicating with my children as I discipline.

If you had to answer with a one on any of these, set a personal goal to make the statement truer of you.

Family Rules. Reflect on your family rules. Take Dan Seaborn's advice and come up with the top five rules for your home. Talk about them, display them, and then live them out.

Chapter Six

The Home as an Emergency Room

Sherry

In him was life, and that life was the light of all mankind. The light shines in the darkness, and the darkness has not overcome it.

— John 1:4-5

Some wish to live within the sound of a chapel bell; I wish to run a rescue mission within a yard of hell.

— C. T. Studd

As a mom, I have found that journaling can be cathartic. At times, I sit down and put my thoughts and feelings on paper, especially when things get tough, the reality of sin presses in, and life feels like it is spinning out of control. During one particularly difficult season, when one of our boys and his friends were struggling, I poured out my heart on the pages of my journal almost every day. My entries often flowed from personal reflection into prayer and back into reflection. I wrote this entry in the summer of 2004:

Yesterday brought bad news. While talking with a friend I found out that some of the boys we are trying to minister to are going down very dangerous paths. These are not just one-time mistakes boys make as they grow up, they are making decisions and heading down pathways that can set the trajectory of their future. It was not long ago that these were sweet little boys playing and laughing in our yard and home. Now they are heading into adolescence and I fear they are making choices that could cost them more than they imagine.

I pray for them. I pray for their parents. I care about them. I desire the best for them.

Lord, protect these children who are not so little anymore. I know my compassion and care for these boys comes from your heart.

The doorbell rings and a small group of young teens come in. I am so happy to see them. "Please come in. So glad you're here." I smile at them, and they greet me, but their faces do not light up like they once did. Sometimes they seem so tired. Too tired for people so young. Hopefully this home is a haven, a place of love and peace. Later, the doorbell rings and still another boy enters. My heart's desire is that this would be a place of rest from the world that calls out their name. May they feel drawn here.

God, you know their names. You call out to them each day. You have a purpose for each of their lives. "This is what the LORD says—your Redeemer, the Holy One of Israel: 'I am the LORD your God, who teaches you what is best for you, who directs you in the way you should go.'"[1] How I long that they will come to know you and follow your plan for each of their lives.

Sometimes I don't see them for days. There are times that my house is not the one they want to come to. I worry that sometimes the light of your presence is too bright for them. May the love that is offered, kindness and even food, keep them coming back.

God, I feel your heart for these boys. You know their pain and brokenness. I can see it and feel it too ... not as much as you can, but I get glimpses. God, please breathe your Spirit into this home that they may see the light and feel the warmth of your Spirit touching each of their hearts. Touch each of these boys who need the hope, joy, and grace that you extend freely.

I hope they know they are always welcome. I pray they know that you love them.

—August 25, 2004

Some years ago Kevin and I heard Pastor E. V. Hill preach at a fundraiser for a community ministry that reaches out to at-risk children.[2] With his booming and passionate voice, Pastor Hill said, "Children should be footloose and fancy free. They should be able to play in safety and remain children all the way through childhood. Sadly, childhood is getting shorter and shorter. These little ones grow up too fast and they face pain too young." I remember talking with Kevin about what Pastor Hill said as we drove home, sensing a fresh commitment to make our home an emergency room where children and adults could come to experience health and healing.

BUILD A NEIGHBORHOOD ER

On September 11, 2001, the repercussions of the Twin Towers falling down, a plane hitting the Pentagon, and a plane crashing into a field in Pennsylvania were felt all over the world. They were also felt on the street where we lived. In the days following the attack, our home was an emergency room for neighbors and friends who were afraid and upset. People wanted prayer. They wanted to talk. One neighbor struggled with fear and trust for a long time after the attacks. Friends needed to gather and process what they were feeling. Our home became a hub of care, grace, and conversation.

Where do people go in your community when personal crisis hits? Where do they gather? Do they see your home as a welcome, open place where they can go when times are hard? The apostle Paul wrote, "Carry each other's burdens, and in this way you will fulfill the law of Christ."[3] One of the best ways to care for people who are having a tough time is simply to help lift their burdens and offer to share some of the weight they are carrying. Kevin and I have lived in a triplex apartment, a parsonage, and on Richfield Court's cul-de-sac. Though each location has been very different, in each place we have made our home an open place where people feel welcome. Neighbors have come for prayer, to talk, to cry, and to find help in their times of need. From child rearing frustrations to private battles with sin, from marriage conflicts to times of deep loss or fear, we've found that God's light will shine and his healing will come if we are open to making our home an emergency room.

How does this happen?

We need to work at it. For our homes to serve effectively as spiritual and emotional ERs in our neighborhoods, we must again remember that the primary care giver is always God, not us. He is the Great Physician. He is the ultimate healer.[4] If we trust in him, serve in his name, and create a place where his grace, mercy, and peace flow, healing will be the natural by-product.

We need to remember that as we walk with Jesus, the love of God shines *through* us. Only God's love is sufficient to heal and restore broken hearts and lives. Why is this so important for us to remember? Because if we forget that it's God's work, we quickly burn out, grow weary, and shoulder the problems of others in ways that are unhealthy and lead to relationships of dependency. Instead of overflowing with gracious love, we begin to resent the intrusions, and we are no longer able to effectively love and serve those in need. The power to heal does not lie within us; it flows through us from God into the lives of those in need.

Be Present

We don't have to put out a neon sign that says "God's hospital." We also don't have to leave our door open twenty-four hours a day to anyone who wants to wander in. But we must be present and available if our home is going to be an emergency room for Jesus. People need to know that we are around. This means we can't drive into our garage, hit a button, close the garage, pull the blinds, ignore the phone, and keep quiet. We need to intentionally be a presence in our neighborhood or whatever place we call home.

Some years ago Kevin and I became friends with a wonderful ministry couple, Randy and Rozanne Frazee. They share our passion for loving and caring for their neighbors and made a deep commitment to letting people know they were available. They intentionally slowed their lives down enough to build significant relationships with others. One of the ways they did this was by simply sitting in their front yard. Many people spend all of their time in the back yard, rarely seeing people in the neighborhood. Randy and Rozanne found that by spending time in their front yard they were able to have many conversations and interactions with their neighbors.[5]

Be Inviting

It is possible to be present but still not be very inviting. Even if people know that you are there, they must also know that they are welcome. The best way to let people know they are welcome is also the most obvious — tell them! Kevin and I have made a habit of meeting and greeting new neighbors when they move in. We bring a small gift and tell them that we would love to connect with them. We invite them to engage as they feel comfortable. We never pressure or push them, but we let them know that our door is open to them.

When we lived in Michigan, a new family moved in down the street, and we did our normal drop in to meet and greet. They were friendly and cordial but very clear that they weren't interested in getting to know us. "We don't really interact much with our neighbors," they said. "If you do neighborhood things, we probably won't be part of them." We appreciated their honesty but suspected that the warmth of our neighborhood might draw them out more. Though many other neighbors and people from our community did engage our invitation and felt very welcome in our home, this family stayed true to their word and interacted very little with anyone else. We learned that we can invite, but we shouldn't force.

Be Confidential

If you want people to feel welcome and comfortable in your home, if you want them to share their joys and hurts, and if you want them to trust you, learn to keep a secret. If someone comes to share a hurt, fear, or struggle, they need to know that their words are locked in the vault of your heart. If you process, share, or chat about the private thoughts that were communicated in the ER of your home, word will get out, and people will never trust you again. The biblical name for sharing trusted information you should not be passing on is gossip, and it is a sin. Guard your mouth and protect the information people share with you. Err on the side of caution when you are not sure if you should be talking about something someone told you within the walls of your house. Keep silent when asked questions by others.[6] Trust needs to be earned. Once our neighbors realized that we could be trusted, it opened the door a bit wider, and we were able to help them in their times of need.

Don't Judge — Be Concerned

As they feel more comfortable and safe in your home, people will disclose struggles, deep pain, hidden sin, and lapses in judgment. Your response is crucial. Don't come as judge, jury, and executioner. Listen, love, pray, and even give counsel if they invite it. Don't beat them up with undue judgment. There will be moments when someone needs to hear a loving word of challenge or conviction. However, our starting point should be grace, not judgment.

People need to look into your eyes and know you care. The old saying "People don't care how much you know until they know how much you care" is a good reminder. We can all dole out advice like a couple of aspirin to cure a headache. People want to know that you still care about them even after they have been transparent and shared their struggles.

Prayer is one of the greatest tools in building a Christ-honoring ER in your home. Pray for a heart filled with compassion and Christlike concern. Be ready to pray for people and with them. Acknowledge who the true healer is so that when restoration comes he will get the glory.

Refer and Get Help

Sometimes you will care for a person in your community and have a very clear sense that you are in over your head. They might need help from a medical doctor, a counselor, a pastor, or some other professional. Don't be afraid to encourage them to get the support they require. We should all be humble and recognize that we can't meet all the needs around us. Some things are beyond our training, expertise, and capacity. Guide the person in need toward someone who can help them take the next step of healing.

PRACTICE PREVENTATIVE CARE

We can faithfully practice preventative medicine, and things might still go badly. Even the best, most involved parents may face seasons when a child simply runs wild and nothing they do seems to help. In these moments we pray, hold on to God, and keep loving our children, trusting that God loves them more than we do. Through it all, we keep doing all we can to make our home a place of healing and health.

Too often we wait to deal with problems until they are critical. My husband has been dealing with minor forms of skin cancer for more than a decade. His doctor taught him to do regular self-examinations so that he can catch little issues before they become dangerous. And we should do the same in our emotional, relational, and spiritual lives. Basic preventative care can help us avoid many of the problems our children, families, and friends face.[7] One of the keys to effectively serving others is making sure that you and your family are healthy first. Here are several practices our family uses to help protect our children from many of the pitfalls of life.

1. Make Time for Family

In a busy world with endless demands, it is easy for parents to overcommit, becoming exhausted and stressed out. Some are so busy they spend very little time at home with their family. And when they are physically at the house, they are often tired or distracted with email, text messages, calls, or take-home projects. One of the best preventative measures parents can take is to carve out time just to be home with their children. This time should be set apart, free of other commitments that divide their attention.

Several studies have tried to determine what brings relational health to a family. Surprisingly, family dinners are more valuable than many people might suspect.[8] The studies found that families who make dining together a priority typically describe themselves as closer and more connected and are less likely to raise kids with destructive behaviors. A study conducted by TV Land/Nick at Nite also affirmed the value of consistent family dinner time. They found that teens who have two dinners or fewer with their parents each week are at greater risk than those who have five or more family dinners each week. Teens who dine less frequently with their families are:

- More than twice as likely to have tried cigarettes;
- One and a half times likelier to have tried alcohol;
- Twice as likely to have tried marijuana;
- More than twice as likely to say future drug use is very or somewhat likely;
- Twice as likely to smoke daily and get drunk monthly.

There are also implications for how parents view their relationship with their teen. The dads and moms who sit with their teens for two dinners or fewer a week were:

- Five times likelier to say they have a fair or poor relationship with their teen;
- One and a half times likelier to say they know the parents of their teen's friends not very well or not at all;
- More than twice as likely to say they do not know the names of their teen's teachers;
- Twice as likely to say that parents deserve not very much blame or no blame at all when a teenager uses illegal drugs.

This study was not done by a Christian research firm — it was done by a television network. If they can recognize the value and need for family time, so should we. Kids are busier than ever with school, sports, clubs, and activities. Some families are so busy that they don't even consider family meals a possibility.

For our family, having regular dinners together wasn't always easy, especially during sports seasons. We tried to accommodate those times by having breakfast together a few times a week. We're not suggesting that your family *must* have five or more dinners together a week or your children will end up in prison. We are simply reminding you that significant face-to-face time with family members leads to healthy relationships. At the very least, parents and their children should talk together every day. Siblings should learn to communicate with each other with respect, honesty, and kindness.

At our family meals we sometimes asked each of our boys to tell about one good thing and one not-so-good thing that happened in their day. This gave them a little direction for conversation. We found that if we just asked them, "How was your day?" the answer was usually a vague "okay." If we invited them to tell us about a thumbs-up moment and a thumbs-down moment, they could share a story. You will need to figure out what rhythm works best in your family. Find time to be together and converse without distraction.

2. Unplug and Tune In

We live in a wired, plugged-in world. The very devices meant to help us stay connected with one another and organize more efficiently often draw us away from our families and distract us from our priorities. A family can be together at home for dinner seven days a week and still experience no communication at all. Dad and Mom are at one end of the table fixated on a large plasma TV screen mounted on the wall. Dad looks away from the TV periodically to respond to a few quick emails from work that pop up on his smart phone. Their daughter responds to several text messages, her eyes locked to her phone's screen throughout the meal. Their son has his ear buds in and is listening to his music.

Though the family is physically together, there are no relational connections, no conversation. Sadly, we're not convinced this is even an extreme example. Often, the reality is far worse. If we are going to get to know our children, we need to go "old school" and turn off the gadgets. We need to turn off the TV, leave the phones in the other room, pull out the ear buds, and look at each other. We need to talk, sharing what's in our hearts, what God is doing in our lives, where we have joys to celebrate and needs to pray for. If we can't do this with our own families, the light of God's love won't shine very far into our neighborhood.

3. Teach and Model Both Truth and Grace

Jesus came to this world full of grace and truth,[9] and this same spirit should mark our homes as well. If we focus exclusively on the truth, we can become dogmatic, legalistic, and overbearing. Yet if we emphasize only grace and never let truth give boundaries to life, we cut our children adrift on the sea of relativism. When we balance truth and grace in our words and actions, we communicate genuine love for others.

When our sons followed the teachings of God's Word, we affirmed them. When they fell short, which they inevitably did (as did we), we extended grace to them, reaffirmed the truth, disciplined as needed, and moved forward together. The balance of truth and grace created a climate for honesty and growth. The challenge was not just teaching grace as a nice theory but extending it in daily life. And with three sons, there were plenty of opportunities to do this.

A PLACE OF GRACE
Nate Harney

Growing up in a small town provided limited options when the weekend rolled around. My friends and I were often looking for something fun to do, and my parents always opened up the house for my friends to come over. They even bought soda and snacks for us! During one of those weekend hang out times, my friends and I were inside watching a movie. It was cold and snowy outside, and everything was slick and icy. Some of us got restless and decided to head outside for a few minutes.

Standing out in the cold, I could see the flickering light of the television through one of the basement windows, and I was immediately struck with a great idea. I decided that it would be great fun to scare my friends who were inside watching the movie by banging my hands loudly against the window.

Without a second thought, I bolted toward the window. I knew that in order to get the loudest bang, I would need to gain some speed. What I didn't realize was just how slick the ground was and how fragile double-paned window glass really is. Seconds later, I found myself *inside* the basement surrounded by my screaming friends. Unable to slow down, I had taken a dive through the window and was now propped atop the TV, covered in shards of broken glass. For several moments, I was in shock, but I was also slightly pleased that I had successfully terrified my friends. Someone ran to get my parents, but they were already on their way downstairs, having heard the screams of more than twenty-five middle-school students.

When my dad and mom came downstairs, everyone was prepared to see me receive a lecture on being irresponsible and to have the party end and everyone be sent home. We had all been to parties where something had been significantly damaged before, and a hole in the wall or a spilled soda on the carpet usually meant the party was over. Surely, a broken window would qualify as "significant damage." When my parents came downstairs, they first checked to make sure I was okay. By some small miracle, I had nothing more than a tiny cut on my bottom lip. Emotionally, however, I was preparing myself to be disciplined in front of my friends.

Much to my surprise, my parents didn't respond in anger. They helped us seal up the window with plastic and duct tape and let the party continue. My friends all commented on how amazing it was that my parents didn't freak out. That next Monday at school, my friends were still talking about it. It left quite an impression on them.

As the excitement over my window dive faded, there was something about that night that my friends never forgot. They learned that my house was a safe place — a place of grace — where it was okay to make mistakes, even big ones! From that day forward, if any of my friends messed up big time, they knew that they could find a listening ear and forgiveness and grace at the Harney house. This was true all throughout my high school years. In fact, even a couple of days before I went off to college, I came downstairs from my room to find my parents visiting with one of my friends. He hadn't come over to hang out with me. He had some serious questions about sin and forgiveness, and he knew that he could be honest at my house and that he would be received with grace. My parents took my window dive and turned it into an opportunity to show my friends that our home was a safe place, one filled with the love and forgiveness of Jesus Christ.

4. Model Good Habits of Health, Exercise, and Rest

Parents give their children a gift of preventative medicine when they teach and model regular exercise, healthy eating, and a pattern of Sabbath. One of my goals as a mother has been to teach my three sons the importance of good eating and regular exercise, primarily by modeling it. The apostle Paul wrote, "Do you not know that your bodies are temples of the Holy Spirit, who is in you, whom you have received from God? You are not your own."[10] As we learn to care for our bodies with a humble awareness that they are the dwelling place of the living God, we develop a healthier lifestyle physically, emotionally, and spiritually.

Kevin has sought to model the importance of Sabbath rest.[11] While he has always taught our boys to work hard at whatever they do, he has also modeled the need to take time to rest. Even though they are all young men now, he still challenges them to take one day in seven to truly disconnect from the regular patterns of life.[12] If you want to make your home a place of health, you can prevent a lot of problems by teaching and modeling a healthy diet, consistent exercise, and joy-filled Sabbath rest.

5. Be on Call

Through the years both Kevin and I have made a point of being "on call" as often as possible. In his years of pastoral ministry, Kevin was always available to our sons when they needed him. Before the time of cell phones, he made sure his secretary understood that a call from one of his sons could always go through (unless he was in a meeting). Now, with the advent of cell phones, the boys have direct access to their dad. They know that Kevin will always take their call unless he is in a critical moment. They are one of his top priorities, and he stays available for them.

I have found my own ways of being on call. When my sons were very young I was able to work at home. Once they were in school, I spent part of my days working at our church, but while working outside the home, my boys remained my first priority. When they were all in junior high and high school, I felt called to quit my job at the church so I could be more involved as a parent in our home. I wanted our home to be a place where kids could hang out, and I knew that my presence and availability were critical in this season of their development.

6. Train for Self-Diagnosis

Parents can be on call, but we won't always be there in times of need. That's why it's essential that parents teach their children how to self-diagnose and how to solve problems as they arise. Refrain from solving every problem for your child; instead help them learn how to figure things out. Ask good questions, give direction, and help your sons and daughters discover that they can come to healthy and God-honoring decisions through their own prayers and study of the Bible.

When our son Nate was in college he found that he loved studying and also enjoyed working on campus. Before he knew it, he had four part-time jobs on campus and a full load of classes. Kevin and I had a feeling he was overdoing it, but we were hundreds of miles away. We knew he had to diagnose the situation on his own.

Nate called us one day, saying he felt he had taken on too much. He already knew something was wrong, so I asked him two diagnostic questions to help him self-evaluate. First, I asked, "Do you have joy in your life right now, Nate?" It was quiet on the other end of the line for several seconds. Then Nate admitted that his joy for life was waning. So I asked him a second question. "Nate, do you have hope?" Again, he was silent for a moment as he reflected. "I think I am losing some hope too." I didn't have to tell him something needed to change. He had figured it out for himself. Nate made appropriate adjustments to his schedule, dropping some commitments, and everything fell back into place. His joy returned, and hope was renewed in his heart.

I still remember Kevin's final words from our phone conversation with Nate that day: "Nate, you have discovered that you have limits. You can push too hard. Next time I know you will consider dialing back before you take on too much. What a great time of life to learn this lesson! It's so good to know when you are hitting the boundaries of what you can manage. This will serve you well in your future." We were both proud of our son that day.

7. Stay Up-to-Date

Good hospitals update their equipment on a regular basis. They mandate that their staff stay current on the latest medical technologies, treatments, and procedures. Parents should be just as serious when it comes to the latest cultural trends and developments. Do an occasional Google search for the top ten television programs and watch a portion of each one. Why? Because these shows often reflect the culture our children are swimming in. You might want to visit YouTube a couple of times each year to view the most-watched videos. These exercises are not meant to be voyeuristic but educational. It's important for parents to stay on top of what is happening in our society. Some of the things you see might break your heart and lead you to pray with greater passion. At the very least, these exercises will help you better understand the world in which your kids are being raised.

CELEBRATE HEALTH

An emergency room home is a place where health is celebrated. When we see our children take positive steps in the right direction, we let them know how proud we are of them. Affirmation can often inspire greater steps toward health. Rejoice when your son says no to peer pressure and makes a wise choice. Celebrate when your daughter decides not to behave like her girlfriends because she wants to honor Jesus.

Another way to encourage healthy behavior is to increase the freedom and personal responsibility you give to your children when they make wise choices. The healthier their lifestyle, the greater their freedom. By the time each of our sons was starting their senior year of high school, they had demonstrated that they were making good decisions. We affirmed this by giving them total freedom. They had no curfew their senior year. We basically treated them as adults; our only requirement was to let us know if they were staying overnight at a friend's house. It was amazing to see each of them treat this freedom with great care. Because they had shown us that they could live as grown-ups, we treated them that way, and in turn they acted like adults. When they went off to college, they weren't drawn to a wild lifestyle with their new-found freedom because they had already been "on their own," making their own choices for over a year. The difference was, their first year of freedom was at home, and we were able to observe how they used it.

In a broken and hurting world, God rejoices when our homes are lighthouses of grace and emergency rooms of healing. This is a gift for our children and a blessing to our neighbors and community. The truth is, we are all broken and in need of God's grace. As we receive God's love and share it with others, our homes become places that draw in those who are broken and hurting. Jesus is the Great Physician, and he is ready to offer healing just like he did when he walked on this earth. The difference is, he wants to extend this ministry through our hearts, hands, and homes. When this happens, grace flows freely and our homes become a lighthouse in this dark and hurting world.

BECOMING A LIGHTHOUSE

Try one of these ideas in your home and with your family ...

Write It Down. This chapter started with a journal entry. If you have never written down your reflections and prayers, give it a try. For a month, make time to write for five to ten minutes at least twice a week. Keep a record of what is happening in your home and neighborhood. Write prayers for the people you care about and the things you hope God will do in and through your home. Make this a normal part of your spiritual disciplines if it helps you focus and process your thoughts.

Be Present and Unplugged. Plan some family time around a meal, in your living room, or in the yard. Make time and space for conversation. Ask everyone to come unplugged from all technologies (it might actually be painful for some kids to put their phone down for twenty to thirty minutes). You can bring a couple of questions, or you might just do a check-in and have everyone share one good thing and one not-so-good thing from their day. Make sure you close your time in prayer. This could feel strange if you never do it and difficult if your family members are used to being plugged in when they are together, but give it a try.

Be on Call. Let your children know that you want to be available and on call for them as much as you can. Talk about how they can get in touch with you if something urgent comes up. Then, make sure you answer or are there when they want to connect (as much as you can).

Get Up-to-Date. Spend twenty to thirty minutes on YouTube watching the most popular videos of the day, week, or year. Make sure SafeSearch is on when you Google. Take a look at a few top music videos. Talk about what you learn from these videos about the culture your children are growing up in.

Chapter Seven

The Home as a Playground

Kevin

Light shines on the righteous and joy on the upright in heart. Rejoice in the LORD, you who are righteous, and praise his holy name.

— Psalm 97:11 – 12

God is pursuing with omnipotent passion a worldwide purpose of gathering joyful worshipers for Himself from every tribe and tongue and people and nation. He has an inexhaustible enthusiasm for the supremacy of His name among the nations. Therefore, let us bring our affections into line with His, and, for the sake of His name, let us renounce the quest for worldly comforts and join His global purpose.

— John Piper

Christians should be the most joyful people in the world. After all, joy is a fruit of the Spirit.[1] We are called to rejoice in the Lord at all times.[2] We can celebrate in even the most painful and trying of times because God is with us.[3] If followers of Jesus are the most joyful people in the world, then Christian homes should be celebrative and happy places, places where people want to be.

Sherry and I have dramatically different personalities. Sherry works at her work and works at her play. She has to make a point of playing. It isn't easy for her to just let go of the responsibilities of life. I, on the other hand, play at work, and I play at play. I love what I do each and every day as a pastor and writer. I have childlike delight in my daily responsibilities. Sherry will sometimes say to me with a twinkle in her eye, "You know you are not normal. I hope you thank God for your disposition." Even though I enjoy my work, I also carve out time on a weekly basis to get away from my responsibilities to relax, rejoice, rejuvenate, and play.

We decided early in our marriage that we wanted our home to be a fun place, a place where people would want to gather. We prayed that one day we would have children and they would love being in our home, and we made an effort to turn our home into a playground. It came a bit easier for me than it did for Sherry, but with time (and some hard work) she has learned to play!

One cold Michigan afternoon we sat on the living room floor playing a board game with our sons. I grew up playing lots of games with my family. Sherry—not so much. As we played, my wife had a pile of laundry sitting next to her, and between each turn she folded a few items in her laundry basket. At one point, one of our boys looked at her and said, "Mom, can you stop folding the laundry and just play the game with us?" Instead of defending herself, Sherry apologized and pushed the laundry away. She worked on staying focused for the rest of the game. Our son reminded her that playtime is not an opportunity for multitasking. It's a time to enjoy being together, not a time for work. We send a clear message to our children when we can't take time to give them our full attention. We also teach them something about our priorities, the need for balance, and what it means to live a life of faith when we make our home a place of play and joy.

A THEOLOGY OF FUN, PLAY, AND JOY

Sherry and I have made it a priority to have fun, play with our kids, and share our joy with the people around us. After our son challenged her to be present, Sherry made a commitment to learn how to be a good "player." We spent countless hours playing an assortment of basket-ball games on our driveway with our boys and dozens of neighborhood kids (and sometimes their parents). We organized football and soccer games on the lawn. We cleared a hockey rink on the pond in the winter when it got cold enough. We hosted and planned all kinds of parties for our neighbors, our sons' sports teams, and groups of friends from school. We had wrestling matches in the back yard and sleepovers in the basement. Why such a commitment to having fun and playing hard? Because the Bible teaches us that God takes delight in our joy.

One of our favorite books for families is *Sacred Parenting* by Gary Thomas. In his book, Gary does a beautiful job of balancing the joy of parenting with the call to let God form and shape us through the experience of raising children.[4] At one point in the book, Gary quotes well-known British author G. K. Chesterton on the gift of laughter and pleasure: "Christianity fits humankind's deepest needs because it makes us concentrate on joys that do not pass away rather than on inevitable but superficial and transitory grief. Instead of getting buried by the seriousness of a fallen world, faith in Jesus Christ offers us the ability to laugh and enjoy ourselves, resting in God's promised eternal joys and pleasures."[5] Chesterton reminds us that we can and should experience delight—the joy of God—even though we live in a broken and harsh world. We may just need to work at it a bit!

In the 1980s, Sherry and I attended a conference in the Bay Area. One of the speakers was Brennan Manning, the author of the book *Abba's Child*, who shared this story:

> There was a priest from Detroit named Edward Farrell who went on his two-week summer vacation to Ireland, where his one living uncle was about to celebrate his eightieth birthday.
>
> On the great day the priest and his uncle got up before dawn and dressed in silence. They took a walk along the shore of Lake Killarney. They stood side by side, not exchanging a word, and stared at the rising sun. Suddenly the uncle turned and went skipping down the road. He was radiant, beaming, smiling from ear to ear.
>
> The priest said, "Uncle Seamus, you really look happy."
> "I am, lad."

"Want to tell me why?"

His eighty-year-old uncle replied, "Yes, you see, my Abba is very fond of me."

Knowing that we are loved by our heavenly Father should bring great joy to our hearts. When was the last time you skipped with delight because you were overwhelmed by the goodness and love of your heavenly Father? Do you believe that God loves you and that he also *likes* you? That he enjoys you, the person he has made, the person Jesus gave his life to save? When we drink deeply of God's grace and swim in the ocean of his unquenchable love, joy is a natural by-product.

Elton Trueblood, in his book *The Humor of Christ*, writes, "Any alleged Christianity which fails to express itself in gaiety, at some point, is clearly spurious. The Christian is joyful not because he is blind to injustice and suffering, but because he is convinced that these, in the light of the divine sovereignty, are never ultimate.... Though he can be sad, and often is perplexed, he is never really worried. The well-known humor of the Christian is not a way of denying the tears but rather a way of affirming something which is deeper than tears."[6]

Christians must learn to strike this balance between shedding tears and having an inner joy through faith that the pain in this world is not the end of the story. We are not blind to the needs in this world, but we are so astounded by grace that joy marks our lives, even through tears.

Some Christians fear their desires, worried that it's dangerous to enjoy life too much. They wonder if what God really wants is for us to dial things back a bit, get serious, and settle down. C. S. Lewis argues that the problem isn't that we desire too much, it's that we don't desire strongly enough what brings lasting joy and pleasure: "If we consider the unblushing promises of reward and the staggering nature of the rewards promised in the Gospels, it would seem that our Lord finds our desire not too strong, but too weak. We are half-hearted creatures, fooling about with drink and sex and ambition when infinite joy is offered us, we are like ignorant children who want to continue making mud pies in a slum because we cannot imagine what is meant by the offer of a vacation at the sea. We are far too easily pleased."[7] According to Lewis, when we really understand the gospel, we are freed to drink as deeply as we want from the well of God's goodness.

God desires for us to walk in joy and experience delight in this life. The apostle Paul declares, "And we know that in all things God works for the good of those who love him, who have been called according to his purpose."[8] In Ecclesiastes we are assured that there is a time for everything under the sun, including times to enjoy the things God provides: "There is a time for everything, and a season for every activity under the heavens ... a time to weep and a time to laugh, a time to mourn and a time to dance."[9] Christians should be great dancers and the best (clean) joke tellers. Even Nehemiah, who knew a lot about hard work and conflict, understood God's desire for his children to celebrate saying, "Go and enjoy choice food and sweet drinks, and send some to those who have nothing prepared. This day is holy to our Lord. Do not grieve, for the joy of the LORD is your strength."[10] Our homes are far more attractive to our friends and neighbors when they overflow with laughter, joy, and fun. A home that feels like a playground can be a sacred place.

HEAVENLY MOMENTS

What are the memorable and sacred times in your family history? For our family they include times of laughter and joy, times when we knew God was present and pleased. Often they involve laughing together to the point of tears. These are heavenly moments.

Sherry remembers a time when the boys were preschool age. They were all together in the playroom, and, in a spontaneous display of sheer joy, Sherry and the boys began dancing and laughing. There is something wonderful and innocent about watching little children dance with freedom and joy. They laughed until it hurt and danced until they were exhausted. Today, Sherry remembers this as a sacred moment.

When our boys were young we had limited resources, but we were committed to creating memories and experiences of joy. We worked hard to save extra money so we could take them skiing. These were times as a family in God's creation, playing together and enjoying God and one another. The beauty of the scenery mingled with the thrill of the sport brought unity and delight to our family. And in these times, God came near to us.

Other sacred moments happened during the day-to-day of life. Our family still remembers when Josh was six years old and we were out at a restaurant for dinner. Josh saw a lemon slice in a glass of water and assumed it was like an orange. We cautioned that it would be very sour, but he assured us that he could handle it. He wrapped his lips around the wedge and took a big bite. We could see in his eyes and face that the lemon was terribly sour, but strained not to let any of us know and would not pucker those little lips. This went on for five or six rounds of lemon sucking. It seems like a silly moment, but it brought fun and laughter to our dinner table. That little boy's face is locked in our memory banks for a lifetime.

Make sure that you are taking time for memories like this. Make sure that you treasure them when they happen. We know that God is present with us, close to us in the hard times of loss and disappointment. But God is also near when smiles brighten our faces, when families laugh until they cry, and when joy flows freely. Joy is a gift from our loving Father, and families that know how to play and laugh reveal that the glory of heaven is present in their homes. Laughter is a sign that the kingdom of heaven is truly among us.[11]

SPEAKING THEIR LANGUAGE

Earlier we mentioned the importance of knowing and studying your children, and this is also true when it comes to fun. Parents must discover what each child enjoys and create opportunities they will find fun. Author Gary Chapman is well known for the study of what he calls "love languages."[12] He focuses on five distinct ways adults and children communicate and receive love:

1. Physical Touch
2. Words of Affirmation
3. Quality Time
4. Gifts
5. Acts of Service

The idea of love languages also applies to the ways we enjoy playing and having fun. While these categories aren't exhaustive, they remind us that each person is different in what they enjoy and how they like to play. What's important is that you learn what connects best with the people in your life. Study each of your children, figure out what shows love to them, and create fun experiences for them to enjoy.

When one of our boys was in middle school he decided he liked coffee. It might surprise you to hear this, but I've never had a cup of coffee before, and I don't plan to start drinking it anytime soon. Sherry enjoys an occasional cup, and she took great delight in going out for coffee with our son on many occasions. Because he enjoyed coffee, this became a special time for them to connect. As we get to know our children we discover how to create experiences that bring them joy and delight.

A WELCOMING SPACE
Josh Harney

Over the years, your groups of friends will shift and change based on your stage of life, priorities, and interests. When I was thirteen years old, I got my first skateboard. I started practicing small tricks on my driveway and cruising around my cul-de-sac. Soon after that I wanted to stretch myself and learn to do more complex tricks.

I sought out the other skateboarders in my middle school and began skating all around town with them. After school most days we would go searching for bigger and better skate spots. Over the next few years, these guys became my group of friends. A few of them were a bit rough around the edges, but my parents would always welcome them with open arms into our home. It was a safe place to hang out, get some snacks, and be in a strong Christian environment.

As skating became more popular, more and more places put up signs that said "No skating allowed." We got chased out of a number of places with good stairs and rails because they did not want the insurance risk or the possible damage to their property.

Around this time my family did something unheard of. My parents paid the money for supplies, and my grandfather built a skateboard ramp in our backyard. My grandpa can build anything, so it turned out very nice. This became a spot my friends and I could hang out. It seemed ironic that in a time when lots of people and places were rejecting skaters, my family not only welcomed them but actually made a space where we could hang out.

THE PATHWAY TO FUN

Because every home, child, and neighborhood is unique, there is more than one way to turn your home into a playground. Here are some of the lessons we have learned along the way, mostly through trial and error.

1. Let Your Children Be Children

Today, children are pressured to grow up quickly while many adults still act like adolescents. I once heard a friend, Ben Patterson, say, "This generation of youth is one of the most unprotected generations in history. They are exposed to way too much, way too early."[13] As parents we are called to help our children enjoy childhood, not pressure them to grow up too quickly.

2. Let Play Be Play

It may surprise you that one of the ways kids lose the childhood joy of play is through organized sports. When children participate in sports, it should be a game, something to enjoy. Sadly, some parents push their kids to play sports year round, hoping that they might get a college scholarship or an opportunity to play professionally. It is great if a child excels at a sport, but play should always be treated as play. We let our boys play one sport at a time, and they continued only if they were having fun. If it became a burden for them, we encouraged them not to sign up the next season. Talk with your kids about their sports and any other activities they are involved in. Help them find joy in what they do for play or encourage them to look into some other kind of recreational activity.

3. Say Yes Whenever You Can

Parents can easily become "no" machines. Their response to a child's request is almost always an emphatic no. Chuck Swindoll's book *The Strong Family* has one of the best pieces of parenting advice we have ever received: parents should say yes as often as they can and say no only when they must. We have lived with this rule, and it has brought joy to our home.

Our sons once asked if they could sleep on a mattress on the floor with no bed frame or box springs. Sherry was reluctant, but we discussed if there was any real good reason to say no, and we could not come up with one. So we said yes. This ended up being a little difficult for Sherry because all three of our boys ended up sleeping on mattresses on the floor for a number of years. For the boys, it was a way to make their room a place where they felt comfortable. The lesson we learned was to put your no's in the bank and use them only when you must. Say yes whenever you can!

4. Focus on the Positive

Ordinarily, Christians should focus on the positive. There will be times you need to deal with tough issues and confront wrong behavior, and when you do, be sure it is done prayerfully and with wisdom. Our normal behavior, however, should be to encourage, bless, and build others up. This includes our children, spouse, neighbors, and anyone who comes into our home. It's easy to find bad things to fixate on, but it's just as easy to find good things to celebrate. If you want to have a home that is a joy-filled place of play, focus on the positive as much as you can.

5. Slow Down

Our culture is pathologically busy, providing little space to slow down, breathe deeply, and be at peace. If we are going to grow a home with joy and fun, we can't do this while driving in the fast lane at a hundred miles per hour. We have to slow down, stop multitasking, and be present with our families. Leave work at the office, literally. Don't bring it home. Turn off your phone while enjoying family time. Before the age of cell phones, a dad went out to play with his child, giving them his full attention. He didn't have email notices beeping or vibrating in his pocket. Slowing down is a choice, and it can be one of the best choices we make for the health and joy of our family.

6. Ask for God's Help

If you are struggling to find joy in your life, try asking God. Joy is one of the fruits of the Spirit. Some people seem to grow this fruit naturally, and they have extra they can share with others. But there are also passionate followers of Jesus who are not as joyful by nature. They need to cry out for God's help. If you are struggling with a lack of joy in your life, start by asking God to help you grow in your ability to play and laugh and experience the enjoyment he desires to share with you.

7. Find Fun Friends

One of the best ways to raise the fun quotient in your home is to infuse your family times with joy-filled people. Identify men, women, and families in your neighborhood or community who know how to have fun. Ask God to use them to bring joy to your family. When we lived in Michigan, our friends Don and Beth Porter always brought laughter when they came into our home and spent time with our family. They love Jesus and have a way of bringing his joy with them wherever they go. When we moved to California, Rick and Veronica Alexander became friends. They always bring a joyful spirit and playful presence whenever they are with us. Having people like this who share in our family time increases our joy.

8. Set Boundaries

Our neighborhood in Michigan was filled with boys. Whenever I played a game in our front yard with my sons, a dozen other boys would appear in a matter of minutes. I enjoyed organizing games and activities for the kids in the neighborhood, but there were also times when I had to draw a line. At one point our sons started asking, "Could we have time to play with you ... without the whole neighborhood being here?" It was a fair request. They enjoyed playing with others, but they also wanted time to be alone with their dad.

I took some time to explain to the boys in our neighborhood that sometimes we would be having "Harney Family Time," a time for playing just with my boys. I was kind but very clear. And I was amazed to see that the boys understood and respected our request. Often, they would see us playing and would call out, "Is it Harney Family Time?" If I said yes, they would ask when it would be time for everyone to play and then come back at that time.

Many of the kids in our development also liked to come over in the summer months because we had an above-ground pool. Sherry set up a day when all the neighborhood children were welcome to come over, if a parent came along with them. The other days of the week were reserved for our kids or for the friends they invited. These neighborhood pool days led to some great times of friendship and ministry with many families from our neighborhood. By setting boundaries, Sherry and I made time for fun with our own family while cultivating opportunities to welcome and interact with our neighbors and their children.

9. Leverage Golden Times

Certain times are better than others for having fun together as a family—we call them the "golden times." We discovered several of these golden times, times when our family was especially eager to engage in meaningful interaction, play, and sharing the joys of the day. For us, this included the morning when the kids were just waking up, meal time, just after school, and right before bed. We encourage parents to do whatever they can to be available at these golden times. Look for ways to engage with your kids, play with them, and enjoy life together in these moments.

Sherry made it a priority to be home when the boys returned from school. She made sure each of them had time to interact with her in a meaningful way that fit his unique style. One of our boys was so social that he would drop his book bag at the front door and take off to see his friends. Sherry made sure he came inside the house and talked with her for a few minutes before leaving. Another son needed the time after school to process the events of the day because of his sensitivity toward others. He would share some of the victories and joys of the day, as well as some of the harder things that he and his friends had experienced. One of our sons is more quiet and reflective. Sherry had to try different things to engage him and teach him how to briefly share about his day. She sometimes asked him to rate his day on a scale from one to ten, ten being great. If he gave a higher number like eight, she would ask, "What made your day an eight?" If he gave a low number like three, Sherry would ask, "What would have made your day a four?"

I gravitated toward the golden time of the evenings, just before bed. It's amazing how three boys are still ready to play and have fun when the clock is ticking toward their bedtime! When I was a little boy, my dad gave me "swings" every night. He would bend over, hold his arms down, and lock his fingers together to make a seat. I sat in his hands, and he would swing me frontward and back between his legs. I did this with my boys when they were young, but then they asked me to spice it up a bit. We started coming up with some new ideas and inventing all sorts of swings. There was the Superman swing, where I would lie on my back and balance each boy on my feet up in the air. Then I would say, "It's a bird, it's a plane, it's Superman," and launch them into the air, onto their bed. We also had the surfer swing, where I would lie down and they would stand on my stomach. I would hum the surf song "Wipeout" and make sure they crashed at the end of the song. We had several others, including the airplane swing, the bouncy swing, and the famous Flipper-Doodle-Do swing. Over the years we developed around twenty different swings, and we had plenty of laughter and fun together.

Turning your home into a playground is great for outreach. It encourages your children to want to be in your home and to invite their friends over. To turn your home into a lighthouse of God's grace, it must be a place of joy. We must remember that God is the author of joy and the Holy Spirit wants to grow it in each of us. Delight, laughter, and play are gifts from a heavenly Father who loves his children. God might not do swings for us before bedtime, but he offers us something far better: unending joy and the knowledge that we are forgiven, loved, and accepted as his children forever. And that's a reason to celebrate!

BECOMING A LIGHTHOUSE

Try one of these ideas in your home and with your family ...

Theology of Play. Have a conversation with your spouse and children about how God views play, joy, and celebration. Talk about how God is the author of joy and how he takes delight when we have fun. You might even want to post a passage like Ecclesiastes 3:1, 4 where you keep your toys or games.

Language Study. Study each of your children and identify what language makes them feel loved and experience joy. When you have a sense of each child's love language, test it out by seeking to show them love in a way that fits their God-given wiring.

Pathway to Fun. Review the nine ideas that can help build a pathway to fun in your home. Identify one that is not a strong suit in your life and set a goal to develop better behavior in this area in the coming week.

Chapter Eight

The Home as a Place of Prayer

Sherry

Then Jesus cried out, "Whoever believes in me does not believe in me only, but in the one who sent me. The one who looks at me is seeing the one who sent me. I have come into the world as a light, so that no one who believes in me should stay in darkness."

— John 12:44 - 46

Your home will become a place of prayer when talking with God is like breathing … we must do it or we die. Prayer is not a routine behavior we execute at a set time of the day with mindless repetition. It is a continual and passionate conversation with the God who loves us and longs to communicate with his children.

— Garth Megargee

It is almost impossible to get a job in this town."

That's what our youngest son, Nate, was told when he moved to Spokane, Washington, to attend Moody Bible College. Classmates assured him that jobs just weren't easy to find in a town with such a huge population of college students.

But this did not discourage him. Nate called us and asked if we would pray for him. He confidently assured us, "I am going to look for a job until I have one." We prayed with him over the phone, and he went out job hunting.

Nate called again a few days later. He was employed! He had secured a job in a fabric shop, to his surprise — and ours. He walked into the store, talked with the manager, and promised her that he would work as hard as he could and give her one hundred percent. She hired him on the spot.

Since I had never been into sewing all that much, I asked Nate, "Do you know anything about fabrics?" He responded with confidence, "No, but I am going to learn." Kevin and I prayed for Nate as we took an evening walk that night, and we thanked God for his provision. We also asked God to use Nate to shine the light of Jesus as he helped people with their fabric orders and as he related to his fellow employees.

Since it's not all that common for a man to work in a fabric store, it led to some humorous interactions. One day Nate called us to share that he had been helping a customer pick out some fabric to make something for her boyfriend. She looked at our son and said to him, "If you were a guy, which of these two fabrics would you like best?" Nate has a sharp sense of humor, and without missing a beat, he responded, "Don't let my apron fool you. I am a guy, and I would go with the fabric on the right."

There were some more serious times as well. Nate shared with us a time when he had a conversation with another employee and she suddenly began asking him questions about God, heaven, and hell. Knowing that Nate was a Christian, she wanted to hear why he believed as he did. Nate talked with her about sin, God's grace, and the offer of salvation given to all who trust in Jesus. By the end of their conversation, this woman, through the gracious work of the Spirit, had responded to the gospel and embraced Jesus.

This is what happens when your home is a place of prayer. Our son had been the object of our prayers too many times to count, even before he was born. Growing up, he learned to pray in our home. The practice and habit of prayer formed and shaped his theology and his understanding of God. And by God's grace, he became a man of prayer. Nate had been praying for God's light to shine through him at his workplace. His family members had also been asking God to move in and through Nate as he worked at the store. And now we saw the answers to those prayers.

As Nate shared this story with us, we were reminded that the angels were rejoicing that day as one lost and wandering person came home to Jesus.[1] But we were also aware that this moment of glory did not come out of nowhere. It was the result of God's answering thousands of prayers for Nate, with Nate, and by Nate over the twenty years of his life. Our homes can be powerful strongholds of prayer.

DEVELOPING A PRAYING HOME

The theology that guides our lives is forged in the furnace of prayer. When we pray in our homes, we learn who God is, and we declare what we believe about him. To develop the habit of prayer, there are a number of things that are essential, no matter if you are a single parent, a couple with young kids, newlyweds, empty nesters, or parents of teenagers.

Having an Authentic Relationship with God

Prayer makes sense only when we know the gospel and have received the grace of God through faith in Jesus. Prayer is not a magic formula or an incantation we use to manipulate God. It is honest and heartfelt communication with a close friend. It's just that this particular friend happens to be the Maker and Ruler of the universe.

Jesus said, "If you remain in me and my words remain in you, ask whatever you wish, and it will be done for you. This is to my Father's glory, that you bear much fruit, showing yourselves to be my disciples."[2] Jesus promises that when we ask, we will get what we want. But notice the basis for this—that we "remain" or abide in Jesus. This refers to a relationship of intimacy, friendship, and connection. People in homes of prayer have this kind of growing relationship with God.

Jesus also tells us that he is the Good Shepherd, and as the Good Shepherd, his sheep listen to his voice: "He calls his own sheep by name and leads them out. When he has brought out all his own, he goes on ahead of them, and his sheep follow him because they know his voice."[3]

Sheep are aware of their shepherd. They can distinguish his voice from the voices of strangers. When they hear it, their heads pop up and they look for him. When they see him, they begin to move. They follow the shepherd. This picture of sheep following their shepherd is a beautiful image of listening prayer. As Jesus' sheep, we are expected to recognize his voice and respond to it. In our homes, we must develop times and opportunities to listen and respond to the call and leading of Jesus, our Good Shepherd. When we practice this kind of abiding and listening to God in a home, we teach theology. We teach our kids that God is real. He cares. He speaks. He is present. Children learn these truths over and over as they are prayed for and as they pray with their parents, and they take this habit of prayer and a confident faith with them as they head out into the world.

Knowing God as a Perfect Father

Our heavenly Father longs for lost people to come home, wandering sheep to follow him to green pastures, and broken lives to be healed. The gospel of John records these hopeful words: "Yet to all who did receive him, to those who believed in his name, he gave the right to become children of God — children born not of natural descent, nor of human decision or a husband's will, but born of God."[4] When we come to God through the sacrifice of Jesus on the cross, we become his children and he becomes our eternal Father.

God tells us that he wants us to know him intimately, as our Abba, our Daddy.[5] This means that we don't pray to a disconnected power, a "prime mover" who got the universe started and left us to figure things out for ourselves.[6] Prayer is communication with God, the God who left his eternal glory to come and live among us, the God who adopts us and calls us his children.[7] We cannot forget that when we pray we talk with one who loves us beyond our comprehension. In First John we find, "This is how God showed his love among us: He sent his one and only Son into the world that we might live through him. This is love: not that we loved God, but that he loved us and sent his Son as an atoning sacrifice for our sins."[8] Our Father loves us so much that he gave his most precious gift, the life of Jesus, to bring us back into relationship with him.

Jesus teaches us about the important connection between the Father's love and prayer: "Ask and it will be given to you; seek and you will find; knock and the door will be opened to you. For everyone who asks receives; the one who seeks finds; and to the one who knocks, the door will be opened. Which of you, if your son asks for bread, will give him a stone? Or if he asks for a fish, will give him a snake? If you, then, though you are evil, know how to give good gifts to your children, how much more will your Father in heaven give good gifts to those who ask him!"[9]

Jesus reminds us, as his followers and friends, that praying to God as a loving, providing, protecting Father solidifies our beliefs. Prayer strengthens our faith and our trust in our Father's love. Our heavenly Father loves us even more than our earthly parents love us. If we have brokenness or pain in our lives because of a poor relationship with an earthly father, prayer is one of the ways in which God shows us that he is different, that he is a loving Father. In prayer, we are reminded of the gospel. We remember that God gave everything for us, laying down his life on our behalf, and that he sought us out when we were lost in darkness and dead in our sins. Prayer reminds us that God loves and values us more than we can dream. Knowing God as our Father brings confidence and strength that is reflected to our family, to our friends and neighbors, and to the world.

Prioritizing Prayer

Families who want to experience the power of prayer must actually pray. I know this sounds obvious, but it is profoundly important. Every Christian believes in prayer, but they don't all actually pray very much because the habit of setting aside time to communicate and talk with God is not normal and natural. It doesn't fit organically into the flow of their life. Many might rattle off an occasional prayer before a meal or a special event, but prayer may not be something that saturates their home and family life.

In his gospel, Mark paints a beautiful picture of Jesus praying. He records that "very early in the morning, while it was still dark, Jesus got up, left the house and went off to a solitary place, where he prayed."[10] The Gospels tell us that Jesus made prayer a priority. Jesus set aside time in his day to be alone with his Father. If the Lord felt the need to commune with the Father and made time to talk with him, how much more do we need this in our lives?

As a parent, you teach your children every time you pray with them. But you also declare something about God and your faith when you do *not* engage in prayer. When prayer is natural, frequent, and normative in your home, God's presence is seen and his power affirmed. At the same time, when life's great moments and times of pain come and go without prayers being lifted to God, the message is just as loud and clear: God is not interested in our lives. Failing to pray or involve God in our lives shows others that we think we can take care of things on our own. A lack of prayer reveals that our trust and our hope are in ourselves. Prayer is one of the most practical and obvious expressions of our faith in God, in his love and power.

Partnering with God

Prayer is never passive. It has been said that "prayer is not preparation for the battle; it is the battle."[11] Every time we pray, something happens, both in the heavenly realms and on earth. Prayer is God's invitation to us to partner with him in accomplishing his will in this world. The apostle Paul reminds us, "For we are God's handiwork, created in Christ Jesus to do good works, which God prepared in advance for us to do."[12] We are made for a purpose, for specific works that God has prepared for us that reveal his glory and goodness to the world. The apostle Paul also told the believers in the city of Corinth, "For we are co-workers in God's service; you are God's field, God's building."[13] God sees us as his partners—his co-workers—and wants us to engage in his purposes for this world. Do you want to know what God's will is for your life, for your family, and for your future? Start on your knees, crying out for God's wisdom and leading. Prayer lays hold of God's power so that we can do the work God prepared for us. Do you want to bless your neighborhood and joyfully partner with God to share his love with others? It all begins with the ministry of prayer.

Acknowledging That Pain Is Real

Prayer must be honest. As we seek God, listen to him, and talk with him in our homes, we need to speak the truth. If we pray only about the good things, we are missing part of the conversation. When we refuse to cry out to God from the depths of our pain, we rob our children, our spouse, and others the chance to be real with us. A home of prayer is a place where pain is acknowledged, loss is mourned, and fear is admitted.

The prayer book of the Bible is Psalms, and within this extensive collection of prayers is a group of psalms called laments.[14] Laments are prayers of transparent honesty and raw emotion, expressions of pain, anger, frustration, and sadness. Why does God, through the inspiration of his Holy Spirit, record so many prayers filled with such pain, loss, hurt, and fear? The answer is clear. This is real life.

Pain is real. Loss comes to all of us.

And God cares.

As we pray with this level of honesty, we teach our families that it is natural and normal to cry out to God in our loss and struggle. We teach them to look to God for strength and hope. When we pray with authentic words, expressing the depth of our pain and fear, we teach others that God is concerned for his children and that he understands what we are going through.

Understanding That We Need Wisdom

In the book of James we are taught another important aspect of prayer: wisdom. "If any of you lacks wisdom, you should ask God, who gives generously to all without finding fault, and it will be given to you. But when you ask, you must believe and not doubt, because the one who doubts is like a wave of the sea, blown and tossed by the wind."[15] Through years of parenting, as I've waited on the Lord and sought to be light in the world, I've often remembered this verse, taken God at his word, and asked him to show me the way. God has wisdom that he offers to all who ask with confidence and trust. In the Old Testament, God assures his people that he wants to help them make good decisions: "I will instruct you and teach you in the way you should go; I will counsel you with my loving eye on you."[16] What comfort this brings to a home!

Too often we try to figure everything out on our own. We live in a day when we can Google our questions and find answers in a matter of seconds. Bookstore shelves are filled with books on any topic you can name. There are TV channels devoted to cooking food, purchasing a home, finding medical advice, doing your finances, and hundreds of other areas of interest. It seems as if all the answers and wisdom of the world are available to us. We can find the help that we need in a fraction of a second with the click of a mouse.

And yet we all know that even with these answers, something is missing. God's wisdom is different from anything we can get from TV doctors, financial experts, and talk show hosts. Even the wisest insights of Bible teachers can't replace the wisdom of God. We are told that God wants us to ask him directly and that he will speak to us, convict us, or grant us insight. God's Word is a reservoir of wisdom greater than any internet search engine can provide. As James reminds us, we need to turn to God in prayer, ask for his wisdom, and believe he will give it.

Fighting the Fight

A very real spiritual battle is raging all around us.[17] The battle is also taking place within us. Prayer is our weapon in this war as we pray against the work of the enemy in the world and in our homes. Kevin and I have prayed over our home and children more times than we can remember. We have prayed for the protection of God's Spirit over our sons. We have cried out for God's presence to rule in our home.

Many of these were prayers we said alone or with just the two of us, but as our boys grew, we invited them into some of these times of intercessory conflict. When praying about conflicts or trials, we tried to have the heart of Jesus, remembering when he said, "My prayer is not that you take them out of the world but that you protect them from the evil one."[18] Jesus prayed that God would protect his disciples from the attacks of their enemy, and we have echoed this cry for our sons as well. The power of God's Holy Spirit in the life of a believer is always greater than the power of our enemy. "You, dear children, are from God and have overcome them, because the one who is in you is greater than the one who is in the world."[19]

As we pray with bold assurance, we live out our theology. We know that God wins. He rules. We remember the gospel, that Jesus destroyed the power of sin and death when he died on the cross and rose again.[20] Praying helps us to walk and live with peace and certainty because we know how the story ends.

If your home is going to be a lighthouse for Jesus, prayer must be central to all that you do. Your children will learn that God is present and that he lavishes us with his love. They will see that God gives us wisdom, that he has won the battles that we face, and that he cares about our hurts and fears. Prayer links us to God, reminding us that we are partners in his work. When prayer is a habit in our home, it shines like a lighthouse with the very presence of God, and people sense that they are safe from the rocks and razor sharp reefs of this world. People in our community will also be drawn to this light, even those who do not believe in God or know Jesus.

WEAVING PRAYER INTO THE FABRIC OF OUR HOME

Your children will primarily learn about prayer from watching you. How do you model and teach prayer in the home? Here are some suggestions from our experience.

1. Be a Person of Prayer

Start with yourself. Ask God to ignite your heart and open your eyes to see his amazing grace and love. Invite the Holy Spirit to work in and through you and to convict you in any part of your life where your heart is wandering from God's holy path. Confess sin and repent of it. Make prayer part of each and every moment.

Don't be afraid to be public in your prayers. It is good for children to see parents deeply involved in prayer and study of the Word. Let your daily spiritual disciplines and authentic relationship with Jesus be obvious and evident to them. Children need examples to follow. Ask yourself, If my child grows up to have a prayer life like mine, would this be a good thing?

WATCHING AND LEARNING
Josh Harney

I can't remember too many specific details from my childhood years, but I can still recall one thing I saw every morning as I was growing up. After waking, if I ventured quietly into my dad's study or walked out onto our back deck, I would see one of my parents studying the Word or in communion with the Lord, deep in prayer. And whenever I would walk by the kitchen sink, I would see small passages of Scripture written on notes, posted above the sink. My mom would often be memorizing or reciting these verses of God's Word.

My parents encouraged each of us to spend time consistently in the Word and prayer, but it was never something that they dictatorially forced upon us. Ultimately, it was left to us to sit down, open up our Bible, and talk to God. So why did I do it? Because they set an example for us to follow. To this day, I do my best to read at least one chapter of Scripture every morning, meditate on some key verses, and spend time in prayer.

Whether or not they will admit it, kids are constantly watching their parents' or caregiver's every move. And like it or not, we find ourselves imitating their behavior later in life. I know that my parents' lives have significantly shaped my own attitudes and behaviors. Thankfully, their love for God was such a natural part of our family. By God's grace, that has been passed on to me and my brothers as well now. I am sure that as the years go by, I will become even more aware of just how much of my life has been influenced by their example.

2. Pray with Your Spouse

Married couples should make time to regularly pray together. Your children should see their dad and mom seeking God in prayer as a couple. Whenever Kevin and I lead a marriage retreat or speak at a conference, we discover that many couples have never prayed together. So we walk them through a simple exercise, showing them a nonthreatening way to start praying as a couple. We have them take two chairs and face each other, sitting toe to toe, knee to knee, hand in hand, and heart to heart. Then we tell the husbands (or husbands-to-be) that they will be responsible for leading in prayer. We often see an uneasiness in the husbands' eyes at this point, so we quickly assure them that it will be easy and meaningful, and it will help them learn to exercise spiritual leadership in their marriage.

We ask the couples to sit quietly, and we tell the husbands to begin by praying silently, thinking about some topics they should be praying about as a couple. Once something comes to mind, he can say, "Let's pray about our upcoming wedding," or "Let's lift up prayers for our families," or whatever else comes to mind. Then we encourage the couple to each lift up brief prayers around this topic. Once they have both prayed at least once about a topic, the husband introduces the other topics on his heart, and they both pray brief prayers on each. Then it is the wife's turn to offer topics. After the couples have prayed this way for a few minutes and have covered three or four topics, we instruct the husbands to say something like, "We lift up all these prayers in the name of Jesus." That's it!

A surprising number of the women have tears in their eyes after we do this simple learning exercise. These women have been longing for an opportunity to pray with their husbands, and the experience releases a flood of joy and thankfulness. Praying together is powerful. If you are married to a Christian, make prayer a normal part of your relationship.

3. Pray for Your Children

Pray that your sons and daughters will love God with all their heart, soul, mind, and strength.[21] Pray for them to love communicating with their heavenly Father in prayer. Ask God for this. Ask God to meet your son or daughter in prayer and draw them into such a deep relationship that they hunger to spend time in communion with the God who made and loves them.

Pray for your child's character to grow so that they look more and more like the man or woman God wants them to be. If you aren't sure where to start, consider lifting up a specific fruit of the Spirit for them until you see that particular fruit growing and blossoming in their life.[22] Pray for your daughter if you sense she needs patience for a season. Pray that your son will have self-control in a relationship. Kevin specifically prays for one fruit of the Spirit for each of our boys daily. It gives him direction on how to pray for them.

Through the years I discovered the power of praying in partnership with other moms. Some of these prayer alliances were informal and involved gathering with one or two women, talking about how our kids were doing, and praying. Others were more intentional. For a few years I was part of a wonderful weekly gathering of praying moms called Moms in Touch (now called Moms in Prayer International). This consistent time of prayer with like-minded women had a great impact on my three boys and me. In addition, I have spoken to and encouraged younger moms through MOPS (Mothers of Preschoolers) International groups around the country. This is also a dynamic and Christ-centered ministry that encourages prayer and supports mothers of young children.[23]

When our boys were younger I often prayed with them before they went off to school. Some days I would say, "I will be praying for you today," or I would tell them a particular item that I would be praying for that day. When they got older, I asked them if there were specific things I could pray for in their lives. Don't be afraid to ask your child about their needs. In addition to informing your prayers, it might prove to be a good way to stay in touch with what is going on in their lives. I made sure to check back with them to learn of any answers to prayer. When God answers a prayer, use this as an opportunity to give glory to God and teach your child that God does answer prayer. Your children will come to understand that prayer makes a difference.

4. Pray with Your Children

It is important that Christian parents not only pray for their children but find opportunities to pray with them as well. This pattern and life-style should continue through their whole life. It is rare for a week to go by when Kevin and I don't pray with one of our three boys about an issue in their lives, even though they are now adults. They often call or email us, asking us to pray.

Be sure to set aside time at meals and before bedtime for prayer. This rhythm of regular moments and places for prayer can be very valuable. Also pray together spontaneously in those moments when a joy is expressed, a need is articulated, or a life situation presents a need. Thank God when your little girl tells you she made a new friend. Pray that it will be a healthy friendship and that God's love will shine through your daughter. Stop and pray with your son when he tells you about trying out for a sports team. Ask God to help him give his best effort, and pray for God's will to be done.

Pray with your children about opportunities they have to reach out to those who do not yet know the love and grace of Jesus. Ask them about the spiritual condition of their friends. If your son or daughter has a close friend who is not a follower of Jesus, spend time praying with your child for opportunities to invite this friend into your life and connect them with other followers of Jesus. Ask the Holy Spirit to shine his light in and through your child. Pray that your son or daughter will be bold and ready to share their story of faith and the good news of Jesus when the time is right.

Because Kevin was the pastor at our church, we took separate cars every Sunday, and I realized that our ten-minute drive would be a great opportunity to pray with the boys. During these drives, I taught the boys that you can pray with your eyes open. After all, the Bible never says they have to be closed. While driving to church, we prayed for their dad as he was preparing to preach. We prayed that our hearts would be open and ready to worship and learn in Sunday school. We prayed for all that would happen at the church that day. As our sons grew up and began driving instead of me, I found it was a real delight to listen to them praying—out loud and with their eyes open—as we rode together to church.

5. Teach Your Children to Pray for Themselves

As you spend time praying with your children, it is important for them to learn that they can lift up their own needs and praises. Help them discover that God hears their prayers, even when you are not with them. We have to be careful that we don't send the message that they need their mom or dad to pray for them for their needs to be heard. It is a great parental joy to see your children bringing their own needs and joys (and the needs of others) before God with confidence that the Maker of heaven and earth hears and answers their prayers.

6. Teach Your Children to Pray with Others

As talking with God becomes a natural part of their life, encourage your children to pray with others. Help them discover the joy of praying with other believers as well as those who are not yet followers of Jesus. They will learn to lead in prayer times by praying often with you.

Suppose your family members have been praying for years that Grandma would come to know and embrace Jesus. She becomes ill, and you go to visit her. Wouldn't it be wonderful if your nine-year-old daughter, thirteen-year-old son, or twenty-year-old daughter could approach Grandma and ask, "Would it be okay if I said a prayer for you?" The worst that could happen is to have Grandma say, "No, thank you." In many cases she will gladly receive prayer from her grandchild, even if she is not sure it will really make a difference. In these moments, God can show up in tender and sometimes powerful ways.

Christians spend a lot of time inviting nonbelieving friends, neighbors, and family members to church. This is a good thing. One of the primary goals of these invitations is that the people we care about attend a worship service or church event and experience the presence, power, and reality of God. We want them to encounter Jesus Christ and feel the presence of the Holy Spirit of God.

When our home is a place of prayer and we organically pray for and with people, God is present. The Holy Spirit shows up. It is good to invite people to church so they can meet God, but when we pray, God comes to us. A house of prayer unleashes the power of God right where we live, and the reality of God's presence can be felt long before people ever step onto a church campus.

BECOMING A LIGHTHOUSE

Try one of these ideas in your home and with your family ...

Partner with God. Prayer is a way of joining in with what God is already doing. There is a wonderful book and curriculum by Henry Blackaby and Claude King that is all about helping people discover where God is at work and joining in with him.[24] Walk around your home and neighborhood and ask the Holy Spirit to give you eyes to see where God is at work. Then commit to pray in partnership with what God is already doing for the next seven days. See if this prayer makes an impact.

Pray as a Couple. If you are married to a believer and do not have a pattern of praying together, use the approach taught in this chapter two or three times in the coming week.

Make Time. Make prayer part of the normal flow of your day. There are times to stop everything and pray, and there are also times to add prayer to what you are already doing. I know that Kevin prays for me every day as he makes the bed. He has been doing this for over a decade. I also know he prays for each of our family members as well as his extended family when he swims laps in the local pool. For years I prayed for my community as I jogged. Now I do this as I walk and hike. Both Kevin and I pray for other local churches as we drive by them. We also pray for revival and a fresh move of God in our community. You can add prayer to your shopping experience, to the time you spend on sidelines at kids' sports events, and to anything you do in the course of your day.

Part Three

TURNING YOUR HOME INTO A LIGHTHOUSE

In section one, we looked at the importance of reaching our family members with the gospel. We do not want to be people who share God's love with our community but forget to lead our own children and extended family members toward Jesus. In section two, we talked about ways in which we can raise our children to love God and live for him. In this third section we will explore ways that we can impact our neighborhood and broader community with the grace and message of Jesus.

We begin by remembering that God has placed each of us exactly where he wants us to be right now. In God's sovereign wisdom, you live where you do so that God can reach people through you. Your home factors in to the strategic plans of heaven more than you may realize. People will be drawn to Jesus as the Holy Spirit works through your family. The conversations you have with people and the things you do with and for them can reveal the presence and power of God. As the members of your family scatter throughout your community each day, remember that God is sending each one of them on a mission to bring the hope and truth of Jesus to a lost and broken world.

This is the great adventure, the journey of faith. In this storm-torn, sin-scarred world, God invites our families to bring his light to people, right where they are.

Chapter Nine

Lighthouse Homes

Kevin

If I say, "Surely the darkness will hide me and the light become night around me," even the darkness will not be dark to you; the night will shine like the day, for darkness is as light to you.

— *Psalm 139:11 - 12*

This generation of Christians is responsible for this generation of souls on the earth!

— *Keith Green*

While Sherry and I were enjoying our honeymoon in the upper peninsula of Michigan, there was a big storm back at our home in Pasadena, California. A huge branch fell from a tree onto the electrical wire that brought power to our little triplex, and when Sherry and I arrived home, we were surprised to discover that our power had been off for most of our time away. Everything in the freezer had melted. The food in the refrigerator was spoiled. It wasn't the welcome home gift we had hoped for!

We called the electric company and learned it would be at least a week before they could get to us. Apparently, we were at the end of a long list of people without power. As optimistic newlyweds, we decided to make the best of it. I can still remember Sherry saying, "This will be a fun adventure. It will be romantic. We can do everything by candlelight!"

She was right.

For the first night, at least.

I woke up in the middle of our second night without electricity with a strong need to find the bathroom. It was pitch dark, and I couldn't see a thing. For some reason, I didn't have a flashlight, and there were no matches available within reach. I tried to navigate my way to the bathroom in the dark.

Bad idea!

Have you ever tried walking in absolute darkness? With the lights on, I would have made it to the bathroom in about seven seconds. Without light, it felt more like seven minutes. In reality, it probably took me no more than a minute, but it was a miserable sixty seconds. I shuffled my feet along the ground and waved my arms in front of me, making sure there was nothing that might hit me in the nose. I knew there was nothing there, but in the absence of light I was acting like someone had sneaked into our house while I was sleeping and randomly hung dangerous objects in my room, obstacles I was certain to hit.

That night, I became aware of the importance of electricity in a way I never had before. We take light for granted when we have it. But when it is gone, we stumble along. We are forced to slow down. We become insecure. If we are not careful, we trip and fall.

I remember that experience whenever I think about the spiritual condition of those who are walking in darkness, lost without the salvation that Jesus offers to them. Men and women, girls and boys all around us are shuffling along through life, trying to find their way. And they need the light that Jesus shines. Often, God uses his people to shine his light, to help others see in some small but significant way that God loves them, forgives them, and has a direction and purpose for their lives.

MAKE JESUS' DECLARATION YOUR OWN

Before we go any farther, we need to be clear on this.

It is not a suggestion.

It is not presented as an option for us to ponder and decide if we want to participate.

It isn't even a hopeful word of encouragement.

When Jesus calls us "light," it is a straightforward declaration. Here is what he said in Matthew 5:14–16: "You are the light of the world. A town built on a hill cannot be hidden. Neither do people light a lamp and put it under a bowl. Instead they put it on its stand, and it gives light to everyone in the house. In the same way, let your light shine before others, that they may see your good deeds and glorify your Father in heaven."

If you are a follower of Jesus, then you are his light in this dark world. It sounds almost irreverent and arrogant if you really consider saying these words out loud. "I am the light of the world." Try it. Right now.

"I am the light of the world."

I know that most people reading this book did not actually say those words out loud. So, I'll ask you one more time. Set down your book, iPad, or Kindle, or push yourself away from your computer for thirty seconds. Take a deep breath and say it out loud a few times: "I am the light of the world!"

Do you feel the weight of these words? Does it feel strange to own these words of Jesus for yourself? Perhaps you recall when Jesus applied this image to himself in the gospel of John, declaring, "I am the light of the world. Whoever follows me will never walk in darkness, but will have the light of life."[1] You might think, "Who am I to say this? Jesus is the light of the world—not me! Surely he didn't mean it when he said that I, too, am light to people."

Let me help you answer those questions stirring in your heart. Remember that you are a child of the living God through faith in Jesus.[2] You are his ambassador in this world.[3] You are God's chosen person through the work of Jesus on the cross.[4] And Jesus was pretty clear when he said, "You are the light of the world." Jesus doesn't lie! When he said it, he meant it. You, along with all who love and follow the Savior, are God's light. Believe it, declare it, and live it. To make our home a place where light shines we need to receive these words of Jesus with an open heart. So what does it mean to say that you and I are the light of the world?

ON A HILL AND NEVER UNDER A BOWL

Since I didn't grow up attending church, I learned most of the popular children's Sunday school songs when I was an adult, as my sons were learning them. And I can remember the first time I heard the song "This Little Light of Mine."

> This little light of mine, I'm gonna let it shine
> This little light of mine, I'm gonna let it shine
> This little light of mine, I'm gonna let it shine
> Let it shine, let it shine, let it shine
>
> Hide it under a bushel, *no!* I'm gonna let it shine
> Hide it under a bushel, *no!* I'm gonna let it shine
> Hide it under a bushel, *no!* I'm gonna let it shine
> Let it shine, let it shine, let it shine
>
> Won't let Satan blow it out, I'm gonna let it shine
> Won't let Satan blow it out, I'm gonna let it shine
> Won't let Satan blow it out, I'm gonna let it shine
> Let it shine, let it shine, let it shine

If you've heard the song before, you know it's quite perky and includes some hand motions. As the children sing the first verse, they wave a finger up in the air like a small candle shining in the night. In the second verse, they cover their finger with their other hand and then quickly pull it away, shouting "No!"

Even though the lyrics are very simple, I love this song. It's a powerful message. The children singing it declare that they will let the light of Jesus shine through them no matter what happens. The third verse is an affirmation that they won't let Satan blow out their light; they will continue to shine God's love to others. Sadly, most of us end up hiding our light under a bushel or bowl, and it never gets seen by others. And as the song reminds us, the forces of hell work against our efforts to let the light of Jesus shine in our lives. Satan will do all he can to cover or blow out the light that shines in our homes.

There are several bowls that Satan uses to cover our homes and keep the light of Jesus from shining to others. In particular, Satan tries to put the bowls of good things, fear, disobedience, and material stuff over the light so it can't shine brightly to those in need.

The Bowl of Good Things

Families can easily get busy doing lots of good things and forget the most important thing. Nothing matters more than the gospel of Jesus. We need to train our hearts and minds to focus on the ministry God wants us to do right where we live.

Sherry and I know firsthand the temptation to get caught up in doing lots of good things, as we often found ourselves tangled up in the activities and relationships at our church so much that we had little energy left to focus on loving and spending time with our neighbors. We could easily spend all of our time involved with programs at the church or hanging out with other believers. Other families might invest their time into sports, academic study, the arts, and other good and worthwhile activities, but they become so involved in these things that they forget to let the light of Jesus shine. They devote an hour to God each weekend, but the rest of the week is filled with the activities and experiences that our culture deems most important.

We're not saying there is anything inherently wrong with church activities, doing well in school, being on a sports team, playing an instrument, or having a hobby you enjoy. These are all good things, and they can even be effectively used to shine God's light to others. More often, however, the good things we love to do can demand so much of our time, energy, and focus that they become a bowl over the light of Jesus in our life. We become so committed to these activities that they fill up our schedule and we don't spend any focused time letting the light of Jesus shine.

The Bowl of Fear

Another common bowl that hides the light of Jesus in our lives and in our homes is fear. Parents often fear their children will be influenced by the world, so they keep them away from those who most need the grace of Jesus. Parents try to buffer their children from certain kids in their community, those who seem mixed up and dangerous. They allow their children to play or hang out only with "good church kids." They sign their kids up for Christian clubs and church sports leagues so they won't be influenced by worldly children.

To be clear, we're not suggesting that parents should throw their kids into dangerous situations so that they can be a Christian witness. We recognize the need to protect our kids. Yet we need to be open to the ways God wants to use our families to reach other children and their parents. We should be open to having nonbelieving families in our homes. We can allow our children to be on community sports teams and in clubs with kids who do not know Jesus. This allows them to learn what it is like to let the light of God shine in and through them. As followers of Jesus, both parents and children are called to count the cost and to sacrifice for the gospel. At the same time, parents are called to protect and care for our children. There is a need for balance here.

When it came time for our first son to begin school, we prayed about our options. Would we home school him, send him to a charter school, sign him up at the local Christian school, or have him attend the public school? After praying, we decided to have Zach attend the local public school. In fact, all three of our boys went through public grade school and high school. We found there were countless opportunities for our boys, and for us as their parents, to minister in the public schools and let our light shine there. The public schools in our area were relatively safe, though still quite secular in many ways. We aren't advocating that everyone should do what we did. We believe God can lead parents to any of the four schooling options mentioned above. However we choose to educate our kids, what matters is that we decide after prayer and that we make sure our children's lives intersect in meaningful ways with non-Christian children in our community. We can't let fear become a bowl that covers the light God wants to shine through our families.

The Bowl of Disobedience

Sometimes we do very little outreach in our community and don't let our light shine because there is an area of disobedience in our heart. When sin controls an area of our life or becomes an accepted part of our life together as a family, it hides the light of Jesus. The Bible is clear that we are all sinful.[5] Every home and every family member battles with sin. We all do the very things we know we should not do.[6] But there is a difference between struggling to resist sin through the power of the gospel and allowing or permitting sinful patterns to rule in our homes and lives. When we allow these patterns of disobedience to control our home, it no longer shines as a beacon of God's love and light to others.

The Bowl of Material Stuff

Our culture is pathologically materialistic. The love of money and desire to accumulate stuff is a national pastime. Jesus knew this would be a temptation for Christians in every generation, and he warned us that it isn't possible to devote our lives to loving money and material possessions and to passionately love God at the same time.[7] If material success and the accumulation of things drive our life, the light of Jesus will be smothered by our possessions. We might grow possessive or protective, afraid to allow the neighbor kids in our home because they might mess with our stuff. If our hearts are not secure in God's love, the desire for material things can become an idol for us, and sharing the love and grace of Jesus is no longer our greatest passion.

LET IT SHINE

How can God shine his light through your home and family? What can we do to knock off the bowls, get out from under the bushels, and keep Satan from blowing out the light? How can we really let it shine?

One of the first ways we shine our light is by living in a way that is noticeably different from those around us. People in our neighborhoods are watching us. They notice our actions, attitudes, and motives. And Jesus tells us that people will see our good deeds. When they see consistent examples of right living in our family relationships, they will recognize that something is different and will have to acknowledge that God is at work. This isn't about being perfect. We simply seek to follow God's Word, do what is right, acknowledge when we fail, and give Jesus the glory. The Old Testament prophet Micah gives us a helpful summary of what God wants to see in the lives of his redeemed people: "He has shown you, O mortal, what is good. And what does the LORD require of you? To act justly and to love mercy and to walk humbly with your God."[8] We should seek to act with integrity, be compassionate when we see others fail, and be known as people who are humble, who love and trust God.

We shine the light of Jesus when we are humble and transparent about our shortcomings. This means that we are honest about our struggles. We shouldn't hide our sins and struggles or pretend that we have it all figured out. Admit that your kids are not angels, that you make mistakes as parents. Never present yourself as better than you are. The Bible calls this hypocrisy. Instead, admit when you are wrong, confess if you've been unfair, and freely talk about being a sinner saved by grace. Humility will make you more approachable and will give you countless opportunities to point to Jesus as the one who is perfect, sinless, and worthy of praise.

In addition, be a person of peace. Many people view Christians as angry, judgmental people who are always at war over something. Christians battle the community, the schools, and their neighbors. They love petitions and are often known more for all the things they are against than what they are for. And while there are times when followers of Jesus need to make a stand and hold their ground, on the whole, we should be best known for how well we relate with others and for how we love the people around us. Jesus indicated as much when he pronounced God's blessing on those who seek peace, saying, "Blessed are the peacemakers, for they will be called children of God."[9] Peace is also one of the fruits of the Spirit,[10] and when we embrace the peace that comes from knowing that God has forgiven us and made us new people, the light of Christ shines brighter.

NOT EVERYONE WANTS LIGHT

As you make your home into a lighthouse, many people will be attracted to your home and to your family. Nonbelieving parents may want your kids to be around their children because they have a good influence on them. People will come to your home for prayer, to be cared for, and to receive the lavish love of God. Some will not even know why they are attracted to your family.

But others will not like that your home is shining so brightly. Jesus made it clear that not all who live in darkness want the light to shine in their lives: "This is the verdict: Light has come into the world, but people loved darkness instead of light because their deeds were evil."[11] We need to be ready for opposition, aware that not everyone will welcome our efforts to bring love, joy, peace, and the grace of Jesus to our neighborhoods. Some will push back against you. Why? Because the light of Jesus emanating from your home will make their sin more noticeable. Every lighthouse home will get mixed reviews. Thank God when people are drawn and blessed by the light of Jesus. When some push back and resist the light, remember that when Jesus walked on this earth, not everyone embraced him with delight either.

Jesus said, "I am the light of the world," and he is! Jesus also said, "You are the light of the world," and you are! Jesus is light in his very being. His light never stops shining. All that is good and wonderful and beautiful—anything that is worthy of praise or worship—originates in him.

We, on the other hand, shine with a borrowed light. God accepts us not because of the light in our lives but because of the light-filled life of his Son, Jesus. When we come to God, asking him to forgive us for our sin against him, Jesus begins to live in us and shine his light through us by the power of God's Spirit. Though the light of God is present in our lives, it can be covered with a bowl, and we must guard against this. We need to make sure that when people see the things we do or receive blessings through our lives, they give praise to God. After all, it is God's light that helps them to see, not ours. Jesus truly is the light of the world, and we who follow him can say, "I am the light of the world." May our homes become lighthouses where the illuminating presence of Jesus is seen and experienced.

BECOMING A
LIGHTHOUSE

Try one of these ideas in your home and with your family . . .

Family Prayer List. Talk as a family about times you have been in a very dark place (literally) and how it felt. Maybe it was scary. Perhaps it caused insecurity or uncertainty. It might have been dangerous. Next, talk about people you care about who are living in spiritual darkness without Jesus. These could be family members, neighbors, friends, or people from your community. Discuss how they might be feeling as they walk through life without the light of God shining on their path. Finally, make a list of these people and begin praying for them at meals, before bed, as you drive through your neighborhood, and any other time you pray together. If you don't pray as a family, let this be the launch pad for this new practice.

Saying It Out Loud. For the next week, try something new when you wake up each morning. Say these words out loud: "I am the light of the world!" Pray about this. Ask Jesus to shine in and through you. Pray for opportunities to let his light shine. Let God know you are ready to reflect his beautiful light everywhere you go through the day.

Bowl Removal. Consider whether any of the bowls mentioned in this chapter are covering the light God wants to shine through your home and family. If you identify a bowl, talk with your family members about one step you can take to remove this bowl and let the light of Jesus shine.

Chapter Ten

The Spirit and Atmosphere of Your Home

Kevin

Blessed are those who have learned to acclaim you, who walk in the light of your presence, LORD. They rejoice in your name all day long; they celebrate your righteousness.
— *Psalm 89:15 - 16*

It's not that God has a mission for his Church in the world, but that God has a Church for his mission in the world.
— *Anonymous*

Storms rage in our world. The news presents shocking images of war, murder, economic instability, political turmoil, and a laundry list of human pain. We are tempted to pull the shutters closed, lock our doors, and wait until the storm passes. Unfortunately, this hurricane of human sin and depravity won't end until Jesus returns.

Our homes should be a safe haven for our families, but they also should be a shelter for people who are mired in sin. When the light of Jesus shines from your home into the world, lost and hurting people will be drawn in, and as you open your home to them, the pain and evil of the world will blow in like a storm. If your home is going to be a lighthouse, you need to be prepared—things will get messy! The good news is that as you love and serve people in their pain and brokenness, God's power will fill you for ministry. The presence of the Holy Spirit and the grace of Jesus will heal and transform the lives of lost, hurting, and wandering people.

We once received a call from the mother of a teenager we had been reaching out to. Frustrated and saddened, she told us that she was heading to the police station to pick up her son yet again. Then she asked us, "Can I bring him over so you can spend some time talking with him?" What do you say in a moment like this?

Another time, I was talking with a woman who was struggling emotionally. Out of nowhere, she asked me, "Kevin, when I die, will you do my funeral?" I felt uneasy. What is she asking, and why is she asking it now? What am I really committing to here?

Once, after a group of teenagers left our house, we found a piece of pornography wedged between the cushions of our couch. How do you respond?

Some people we've tried to love and serve pulled away from us once they shared their struggles and secrets. One mother grew angry with us because she did not like the advice we gave when she asked for counsel in dealing with a rebellious child. The list could go on and on. Making our home a lighthouse of God's healing grace has demanded more than we ever imagined it would. And by opening our hearts to let God's light shine, the storms of sin in the lives of hurting people have entered our home.

Sherry and I have opened our arms to our community for almost three decades. We've felt the bitter winds and the pelting rain of the world's storms come blowing into our home, but we've also felt the sustaining power of the Holy Spirit come in like a mighty rushing wind. By God's grace, we have watched as broken people are healed, marriages strengthened, wandering people directed, and lost people found by the grace of Jesus.

Through the mess, God's majesty has been revealed. In the storms, the Spirit of God has sustained us. It has been frightening at times, but also very exciting. We've sought God for wisdom, strength, protection, and resources we didn't have. And in every case, God has shown up and proven himself faithful.

When we were first married, we didn't know if we would ever have a house of our own. Sherry prayed that if God provided us with a house, we would use it for his glory. One day, she sensed the Spirit asking, "What do you want in a home?" So Sherry asked God for three things: (1) a place with space to invite others in, (2) a home of moderate means, nice but not so nice that people would feel uncomfortable, and (3) an area that our family would feel safe in. God answered that prayer. When we moved to Michigan, God provided a house that met those exact three needs. This home in the small town of Byron Center became a hub of ministry and a place where God touched many lives. When we moved to California, we prayed again, and once more God provided us with a home where we are able to minister to the needs of others. We are thankful that our homes have been a lighthouse, even with all the challenges we've faced. As we look forward, we know that wherever we live, we want to continue being a lighthouse home for our neighbors and for our community. There is no better way to live.

We believe that God wants each of us to use our home as a place of service for the glory of Jesus. Most people think of their home as a retreat from the world, and our homes should be places of rest. But our homes must also be mission centers, places that God can use to reach into our communities and neighborhoods. This means that our homes should be inviting places. To make them inviting, we need to consider both the atmosphere of the home and the way we use the physical space.

THE ATMOSPHERE IN YOUR HOME

God's love is the bedrock and foundation of a lighthouse home. Love must be ever-present if we are going to weather the storms outside and inside of our home.[1] Sadly, some Christians get confused about the topic of loving the world. In the first letter of John we read this pointed exhortation: *"Do not love the world* or anything in the world. If anyone loves the world, love for the Father is not in them. For everything in the world — the lust of the flesh, the lust of the eyes, and the pride of life—comes not from the Father but from the world. The world and its desires pass away, but whoever does the will of God lives forever."[2]

The passage calls Christians to refrain from loving the world or anything in it. Some might interpret this to mean that we should lock our doors and refuse to host "worldly people." But then we read something that sounds very different in the gospel of John: "For *God so loved the world* that he gave his one and only Son, that whoever believes in him shall not perish but have eternal life."[3]

So which is it? Is the Bible teaching us that God loves the world, but we should not? The answer is yes *and* no. In his letter, John warns us to refrain from falling in love with the sinful systems and enticements of the world. We are never told to stop loving the people in the world. In his gospel, John reminds us that God loves the world. God loves sinful, broken, and hurting people and calls us to love these people of the world, but not the sinful temptations the world offers. As followers of Jesus, we are expected to love God with passion and devotion.[4] We are to love believers in the family of God and show grace and compassion to them.[5] In addition, God wants us to love those who are like wandering sheep and need to know the love and grace of the Good Shepherd.[6] People will be drawn to God's presence when this kind of love fills our hearts and homes.

Humbly Loving Broken People

Where do we start? How do we create an atmosphere in our home that communicates love for sinful, broken people? We begin by humbly accepting that we don't have all the answers to the problems that people face. We are not perfect. As Christians, we have struggles, pain, and heartache just like everyone else. Our homes are more attractive to those who are far from God when we realize this and admit it openly. Unbelievers will immediately turn away from the stench of hypocrisy, but they will be drawn by the fragrance of humility.

A neighbor once sat down to talk with Sherry about becoming a better parent. The woman was very kind and spoke affirming words about how Sherry was mothering our boys. She had a deep desire to be a great mom and asked for Sherry's advice. Sherry's first response was not to give her a list of parenting tips, as if we somehow had discovered the secret to raising perfect, obedient children. Instead, Sherry admitted that we don't have what it takes to raise our children the way we should, that we quickly come to the end of our abilities and need to cry out to God for strength and power to continue. My wife shared how she looks to God every day for help in raising our boys and how the wisdom of the Bible guides her on every twist and turn of the parenting road.

Our neighbor was very surprised. She had assumed that Sherry had parenting all figured out, that she was an expert in raising good kids. But far from being disappointed by what Sherry shared, our neighbor actually felt closer to her when she realized that Sherry also struggled and needed help. She heard an admission of need and dependence that as parents we look to God, his Word, and his people for help. And she was inspired to look to God as well. Following their conversation, Sherry prayed with our neighbor as she recommitted her life to Jesus and began a new season of walking with him.

Sherry went on to share some practical advice and help her with parenting challenges. But it was clear to both of them that these insights were not Sherry's own; they were based in the truth of God's Word. Honest humility helps people to see that we are not the answer to their needs, that we too are dependent on Jesus and look to him for help, trusting in his provision and kindness.

Sharing God's Wisdom

Wisdom comes as we understand God's plan for life and follow it. A wise person looks to the Word of God and listens to the still, small voice of the Holy Spirit.[7] We live in a wisdom-starved world filled with people who long for direction, clarity, and truth, and we have often seen opportunities to bring godly wisdom to the families in our community. As personal computers became more common in homes, we heard parents talking about the internet, the potential pitfalls of pornography, and other dangers that come with spending time online. While many of our conversations were with Christian parents, some were with those who were still spiritually seeking. They needed help with their parenting, but they didn't know where to turn for wise counsel.

These questions and concerns gave us an opportunity to share some biblical wisdom about purity. All of the parents we talked with had a common desire—they wanted their children to keep their hearts, minds, and bodies pure. This was true even of those who did not embrace the Christian faith. Sherry and I encouraged them and gave them some practical suggestions on avoiding temptation and living with purity. We talked about some of the ways we had applied God's wisdom on this topic: using parental controls and reporting programs (which were very new at the time) and choosing the best location in the home for placing a computer. We shared how none of our boys had computers in their rooms behind closed doors. One family, whose computer was in the corner of the basement, a place where internet use was difficult to supervise, asked if I would come over to help them move their computer to the living room. I helped them set up parental controls, and we had a great conversation about protecting kids from the enticements of the world.

Over the years, we had many conversations like this with our neighbors. We helped people apply biblical wisdom to their parenting, gave advice about dating, assisted people in managing their family finances, helped resolve marriage conflicts, ministered to people going through divorce, and gave practical advice on disciplining children and setting up family rules. We found that people all around us were searching for direction. Often, they would be attracted by the light of God in our home and would have questions for us. They were looking for wisdom for their own lives.

Communicating Warmth and Kindness

One of the most practical ways to create an atmosphere that communicates love to people is simply to treat them with warmth and kindness. Smile, laugh, and welcome people when they stop by for a visit. Your home should be a warm, welcoming place. We can still picture the faces of the many kids and teens that walked through the front doors of our homes throughout the years. We would watch them relax, begin to smile, and find joy once they were inside. Often, they came in with heaviness on their heart, covering them and dragging them down like a wet quilt. But once they were in our home, they warmed up and their hearts seemed to soften. Simply by showing them kindness and communicating warmth through a welcoming smile, we were able to ease some of the heaviness in their hearts.

In addition, we practiced hospitality. We hosted parties at the end of sports seasons, birthdays, Christmas, Fourth of July, graduations, and any other reason we could find. Sherry used the time of preparation as an opportunity to pray for the people who would be attending, silently praying for our guests while peeling the potatoes or scrubbing the kitchen floor. I remember when we were able to invite a coach to our church during one of these parties. He started attending, and it wasn't long before we saw him helping out in our youth ministry.

Our neighbors also jumped in on this, and we all worked together to plan community parties. We had progressive dinners with groups of our neighbors, and these were significant times of connecting and bringing us together. The important thing to remember is that these celebrations do not need to be fancy or expensive, though sometimes they can be. Simply invite people over, have a good time, and celebrate life. When our homes have a reputation for being places of parties, fun, and festivity, it says something about who we are as Christians and the God we worship. At the very least, it shows nonbelievers that we know how to have a good time!

AN OPEN DOOR
Zach Harney

Growing up in our home was like having a huge extended family around the world. Whereas most families only have visitors when relatives come into town, our home was constantly bustling with new people. Very rarely did they stay for more than a couple days, which was sometimes a relief and other times very saddening. It was always interesting. If there was one thing to be said about our home, it's that it was welcoming. My mother always made the guests feel as comfortable as if they were in their own home, and it was a joy to hear people say that they could truly relax and rejuvenate while they were with us. This was true for not only local friends and neighbors but also those coming from around the country and the world.

As kids, having new faces in our home became a point of normalcy. The array of different people was stunning, and I am absolutely sure that the exposure to so many diverse individuals helped shape me into the person I am today. I remember a top-level leader and missionary from Sri Lanka named Ajith Fernando sitting down with me and helping me with my comparative religions homework for school. I will never forget the time I was able to invite a bunch of my football friends over to talk with Ricky Bolden, a former Cleveland Browns player, when he was at our home. Most important, though, I will always be shaped by the many pastors, missionaries, and Christian friends who shared stories of their own walks with Christ and prayed with our family.

The question remains, how was this environment fostered and sustained? While there are many different factors that probably contributed to this atmosphere, I think it really boils down to one simple truth: they felt comfortable in our home. We never treated our home like a pristine museum. We did not force silly family rituals or rules on guests. We never expected people to know assumed behaviors or adapt to our culture. However, we always invited them to be a part of our family and extended as much love as would be received. I believe this is what turned our home into the warm and welcoming place that it was for all who walked through the door.

If people feel they are in a sterile and unwelcoming place, they probably won't come back. If they feel as if they are being ostracized by strange rituals that are not explained, they won't feel at home. Finally, if people are expected to change in an instant and drop everything they know, they will flee and not look back. However, if people are accepted and received as they are, with love and a warm atmosphere, they will be in a perfect place to experience God's love. It will be a place where we actually desire to invite others. Most important, it will be a place that emanates Christ's love, which is exactly what Christians are called to do (John 13:35).

THE PHYSICAL SPACE IN YOUR HOME

The physical space of your home matters. Why? Because the environment in which you spend time with people also helps create an inviting atmosphere. Any size space can be made to feel inviting—it just takes some creativity!

Clean and Comfortable

For the first couple of years of our marriage, we were broke. We lived in a cramped little triplex in a very tough part of Pasadena. A unit in the duplex next to us had been burned out and gutted. There were always three or four broken-down cars parked along the side of the house. Our neighbor, a very sweet guy, spent most of his time in the front yard drinking cheap wine and sitting on an old paint bucket, chatting with people who were walking by. We could have just felt embarrassed and avoided inviting people over. Instead, we decided to clean our place up. We did some work on the yard (which was basically hard-packed dirt) and made our little home as inviting a space as it could be. We had lots of people over to our home, and God did great ministry there. It didn't look all that impressive, but it was a lighthouse. And when we moved to an apartment complex and then a parsonage, we had the same mentality. We tried to keep things as clean and comfortable as we could. We looked for creative ways to keep the space tidy and make it conducive to company.

Strategic Space

When we purchasing our first home, we wanted a place that felt clean, nice, and inviting, but not so nice that people would feel awkward or uncomfortable. We chose a carpet style and color that would mask dirt stains because with three boys and their friends (and Michigan winters), we didn't want to be constantly worrying about people taking off their shoes. We designed our backyard space so that it was kid-friendly. We put in an above-ground pool, a trampoline (dug in to be level with the ground with an adjustable basketball hoop next to it for slam dunk contests), a swing set, and even a place for kids to skateboard. We had strict rules for the use of these areas, but our goal was to make our home a place where kids would *want* to come. Ironically, the only accident we ever had in our backyard happened when one of our boys' friends answered his mother's check-in phone call while still jumping on the trampoline. He fell over and sprained his ankle, but at least he was able to let his mother know that he was fine!

When we first bought our house, we couldn't afford to finish our basement, so we cleaned it up and made it a place where the boys could play street hockey inside. Later, when we could afford it, we finished the basement and designed it to accommodate large groups of kids. We put in a fridge and a place for snacks and implemented a serve-yourself policy for any young people who came over. A refrigerator filled with an assortment of drinks and plenty of snacks is always a good way to make kids feel at home! Anyone who came over to our home knew they had total access to anything in the basement refrigerator and food cupboard. If you don't have a basement, you can use your garage just as well. The key is to creatively think about using the space for outreach, not just for your family activities.

Plenty to Share

My dad's mother, one of the few people in my extended family who had a relationship with Jesus, always invited people over to her home for dinner. Granny was famous for making a dinner for six people and then miraculously stretching it out to feed twelve when guests just showed up unexpectedly. I learned from her example that you can let God's light shine by simply letting people know that you have plenty to share. Even when we were struggling financially for several years, we always made it a priority to share with those who came into our home.

One practical way to prepare for spontaneous hospitality is to stock up on supplies for food that can be easily prepared. We found that our boys' friends loved staying overnight. Sometimes a group of boys ranging in number from three to ten would stay over at the last minute, but Sherry was always ready to make them as many pancakes as they could eat in the morning. She prepared for times like this by finding boxes of pancake mix and bottles of syrup for a dollar each at Aldi, and she kept a ready stock in case she was called upon to feed the masses. We also bought two-liter bottles of generic soft drinks and kept them in the basement fridge. When chips were on sale, Sherry bought extra. We tried to always have food for one or two inexpensive meals on hand, just in case. We even had a line item in our family budget for ministry food. We made it a priority, and because we were prepared, hospitality became more natural and organic for us. We weren't as concerned about people staying over or inviting people to last minute meals. When people were in our home, we could be generous.

Count the Cost

There is always a cost to opening your home in this way. Having large groups of boys staying overnight, hosting parties with thirty middle-school students, and having high school students dropping in at odd times can lead to a good bit of wear and tear on a house. We learned this early, and often! Just after we finished our basement, our boys and some of their friends played with some "airsoft" guns that shoot little plastic balls. We let our sons play with them in the basement during the winter months, and when their friends discovered this they wanted to bring theirs. We didn't realize until after they left that one of the boys had a newer gun that shot like a machine gun and left hundreds of dents in our new drywall, wood trim, and cabinetry. How would you respond? Obviously, we made sure they did not play this game in the house anymore. But that was all we did. We decided to live with dented drywall and marked up wood and counted it as part of the cost of ministry. Thankfully, it was obvious only if you looked really closely.

Over the years, we've paid for repairs to the vinyl side of our pool, fixed broken windows, replaced carpet earlier than expected, and made lots of other repairs. All of this is just a natural and normal part of being a lighthouse. And although the financial costs have added up over time, the stories of changed lives have been of far greater value. It's been worth it.

NOT ALWAYS AN EASY ROAD

I have taught my sons, several friends, and a number of church interns to snowboard. I always tell them that if they are going to learn to snowboard, they will "pay the price." I explain that they will fall many, many times as they learn and that these falls will hurt. If you want to learn to glide down a snow-covered hill on a board, you *will* spend time on the ground. No one learns how to snowboard without some bumps and bruises.

The storms in our world are getting more severe. As you shape your home into a space that is inviting and exudes a warm, welcoming atmosphere that reflects the loving presence of God, know that you need to be ready. Brace yourself. When you open up the shutters and doors during a storm, lots of debris will come blowing in. Yet even though this creates a mess, God's grace can bring calm to the storm. God's glory is often revealed as he cleans up the mess the storm has left.

As you partner with God to turn your home into a lighthouse, you will need to count the cost, prepare for the storms of the world to blow in, and get ready to share what you have with people who need to see that Jesus is alive in this world. You will also get to have fun, see God impact lives, and feel the Holy Spirit work through you in new and amazing ways.

BECOMING A
LIGHTHOUSE

Try one of these ideas in your home and with your family . . .

Cleaning Project. Set aside a time as a family for a cleaning day in your home with the express purpose of making things nice and ready to invite people who are not yet followers of Jesus into your home. Once you have things cleaned up, extend an invitation.

Budget Time. Look at your family budget and add a line for purchasing food and snacks for entertaining people from your community. If you don't have a budget, work on making one and be sure to include an "Entertaining Community Members" line.[8]

Wisdom and Knowledge. We don't have the wisdom that people in this world need. Only God has it. If you don't spend regular time reading and studying the Bible, make this a priority in the daily rhythm of your life. This will prepare you to share God's wisdom with others. There are a number of excellent free reading plans on a website called Bible Gateway.[9]

Chapter Eleven

Connecting in Organic Ways

Sherry

Arise, shine, for your light has come, and the glory of the LORD rises upon you. See, darkness covers the earth and thick darkness is over the peoples, but the LORD rises upon you and his glory appears over you. Nations will come to your light, and kings to the brightness of your dawn.

— Isaiah 60:1–3

We are debtors to every man to give him the gospel in the same measure in which we have received it.

— P. F. Bresee, founder of the Church of the Nazarene

As my boys grew up, I learned a number of new languages. I did not have to study Spanish or French to understand my boys, but I did have to learn the vocabulary and culture of many new worlds. For instance, I was immersed in a new culture and learned the language of soccer when all three boys played the sport for over a decade. I learned the meaning of words and terms such as midfielder, juggling, crank it, throw in, corner kick, striker, bicycle kick, header, and many more.

Through the years I discovered that to connect in my children's world in organic ways meant learning about the culture they lived in and studying the languages of things such as soccer, tennis, Pokémon (a kids' video game and set of collectable cards), skateboarding, and grind-core bands. Parents who want to reach their children with the grace of Jesus and be part of God's ministry to their community need to become students of youth culture and the many subcultures in which their children live.

In his timely book *Youth Culture 101*, Walt Mueller gives a helpful image of the impact culture has on our children. He points out that culture is the soup in which our children soak every day. This cultural stew includes values, attitudes, behaviors, media, and language. If we want to know who our children are, we must learn to lift the lid. According to Mueller, "We can't escape the reality that those elements — as strange and frightening as they may seem — shape their worldview and govern their lives. We might be tempted to close the lid because we don't like what we see. But if we hope to effectively protect our kids from harm, provide for their well-being, and lead them to a vital faith in Christ, we must understand their world ... a world that's very different from the world we knew when we were that age. In fact, the cultural-generational gap between adults and teenagers widens every day."[1]

Our children need parents and other caring adults who consistently work hard to stay in touch with the youth culture to guide them through the maze of growing up. Mueller encourages parents in five ways:

1. It is never too early to learn about the world in which your children live, and it is never too late to get started.
2. It won't be easy, and it takes diligence and commitment.
3. Pain can be a blessing, so stay engaged and don't quit when it gets hard.
4. Understanding youth culture equips you to pass on your faith.
5. Studying youth culture helps foster relational closeness with your children and their friends because you won't seem like a complete foreigner.

As we study the culture and become aware of what is really happening out there, we might grow discouraged and be tempted to stick our heads in the sand and ignore our cultural situation. But this isn't an option for those who want to have a lighthouse home. Part of shining the light of God's love is being involved in his mission in the world, engaging with the people in our community.

CONNECTING IN YOUR COMMUNITY

Christians can engage with the spiritually disconnected in many places and on many levels. One of the first decisions we made to engage our community was to involve our sons in the community soccer, football, basketball, and baseball leagues. We chose not to put our boys in church-based sports programs or special Christian sports clubs, even though there were many available in our community. The hours we spent on the sidelines with other parents provided very natural times for us to relate with people in our community. It also opened the door for us to minister to people in times of need and share about our life and faith. Kevin even coached several of these teams and made the sports experience fun and rewarding for the children on the team. I interacted with parents as I scheduled snacks, threw team parties, and organized all the team schedules. Some of our best opportunities to engage the people in our community came through our sons' sports.

SERVING AND SOCCER
Nate Harney

I grew up playing soccer and loving it. I cannot think of a single game or practice when my dad was not there. In our town, parents could volunteer to be an American Youth Soccer Organization (AYSO) coach. Even though it was not always easy to find coaches who would give their time and energy every week, year after year, my dad would volunteer to be our coach. When he coached, he always gave one hundred percent.

After playing for a couple of years, I found that many of the kids I knew at school wanted to join our team. We certainly did win a lot of games, but the reason so many kids and their parents wanted to be a part of my dad's teams was because of the atmosphere he created. We worked hard, but we also had fun. My dad challenged and pushed us, but most of his time was spent encouraging, not yelling. He would reward us for wins or significant accomplishments by taking us out for pizza or ice cream. My mom was involved providing snacks at halftime or organizing the other moms to help. And when I started playing on our high school team, my parents were always there to assist in any way they could. My mom continued to provide help with snacks and organization, and my dad helped out at some of our practices, even substituting as the head coach when they needed him.

My parents' involvement in my soccer teams throughout the years taught me an important lesson. My parents cared about the sports teams I was involved in, but I knew that they were also doing something bigger. They were purposefully getting involved in our community in order to be a light to others. After years of watching my dad coaching from the sideline and my mom bringing snacks to games, people started to notice that something was different about my parents. I watched my dad and mom interact and form relationships with people who would never step foot in a church building. In other words, *my parents were bringing the church to the people*. On the sidelines of our soccer fields, at school functions, and all around our neighborhood, God was using my parents to show and tell the good news to those who might never hear it elsewhere.

Not only did the boys play sports, but Kevin joined a soccer league just to meet more adults in our community. This opened the door for wonderful friendships and new relationships with people who needed to learn of God's grace and care for them.

Schools and Community Organizations

As we mentioned earlier, we know that loving Christian parents can choose many options for their children's education. Home schooling, charter schools, private schools, and public education are all valid options that can be prayerfully considered. Kevin and I have friends who have chosen each of these with confidence that God was leading them. There are many factors that can and should affect decisions regarding your children's education, such as the culture of your community, the types of teachers your children will have, your child's personal needs, and the overall condition of the public schools in your area. We believe each family must pray and seek the Lord's direction. Kevin and I also encourage Christian adults to respect the choices of other parents and not impose their convictions about schooling on their Christian friends.[2]

For us, the public school system was where we felt God most clearly leading us. The public schools our kids attended were fairly safe and offered a solid education, and by God's grace, our sons were a witness to Jesus in their schools. The public school system was the right place for our family, and for those parents who feel called to choose public schooling, this can be a wonderful and natural place to engage with others. The key is to begin with a humble servant's heart. Pray faithfully, encourage often, and do all of this in partnership with your children. See this as a joint ministry that you can do together.

During our sons' school years, our involvement in the public school system grew. We introduced ourselves to every teacher our sons had and let them know that we were available to help in any way and that we would be praying faithfully for them and their class. Most of them appreciated this. I went to many of the class parties and helped the teachers at these events. Knowing that teachers and administrators are often underappreciated, I used Christmastime as an opportunity to show our gratitude to them with small gifts. Kevin substitute coached some of the varsity soccer games when the head coach had urgent family needs to attend to. We served at a number of the senior all-nighter graduation parties. Kevin even had several teachers phone him and ask if he could be available to counsel parents who were struggling in various ways. This opened the door for some great ministry to nonbelieving parents in the community.

One high school teacher put some of Kevin's books on their optional reading list. On a number of occasions, Kevin was invited to career day at the grade school and high school to talk about what a pastor does. To top it off, Kevin was invited at the students' request to preach at each of our three sons' baccalaureate services. When Nate was graduating, the students also invited him to join Kevin in preaching the message at this worship service. This was the first time in the school's history that the students had asked a graduating student to give the message, and it was a real honor. The public schools in our town were a place of connection, friendships, and ministry for our family.

Even if your children aren't attending public schools, there are other civic organizations, clubs, and community gatherings that you can get involved with. Many of the members of our church in Michigan served in local city government. Every time we went to vote, more than half of the people serving at the polling place were from our congregation. You might also consider joining a local theatre troupe, a vocal group, a golf club, a bowling league, or a running group, just to name a few options. While some churches try to develop Christian "substitutes" for these activities to encourage Christian fellowship and build friendships with other believers, we have found that it is usually better for Christians who want their light to shine to jump into an existing community gathering or program. Instead of trying to convince a non-Christian to join your group, which can be quite intimidating, try meeting them in a place that is more natural for them. By creating a Christian version of these gatherings, we lessen the potential for evangelistic impact.

Where You Eat and Shop

Though there are plenty of options for eating out and shopping, our family tried to regularly dine and shop in the same places so that we could build friendships and connections with the people working in those businesses. One of our favorites was a little restaurant run by a couple who eventually became dear friends of ours. We had a chance to share our faith with them often, and God forged a wonderful relationship between us over the years. Kevin also had regular opportunities to pray with employees at the gas station near our house. They knew he was a Christian, and Kevin made a point of lingering at the cash register when business was slow. The counter at this gas station became a place of ministry.

Kevin did a lot of his reading and studying at a local sandwich shop, and over the years this led to dozens of spiritual conversations with the employees. I can still remember the day Kevin came home and excitedly told me that he had shared the gospel with a young woman while she was making him a meatball sub for lunch. You never know what opportunities God will provide for you, or when they will happen. When you shop and dine at the same businesses, over time these can become places where God's light shines through you.

RESTAURANTS AND RELATIONSHIPS
Josh Harney

I have vivid memories of all the different restaurants our family would go to on a regular basis as I was growing up, from the satisfying Mexican food of Carlos O'Kelly's to the endless Chinese buffet of one of our local favorites, Peking Inn. I would always look forward to these meals, anticipating what I wanted to order and all the different tastes and smells I was about to enjoy.

Through these frequent trips to our favorite restaurants I began to notice that as we came back to the same restaurants on a regular basis, both my parents began to form relationships with the owners and waiters. I saw my mom begin to have a relationship with several of the female workers at Peking Inn, talking about their children, and just catching up with what was going on in each other's lives. At Carlos O'Kelly's, I remember my dad slowly getting to know most of the wait staff in the restaurant and talking with them about our family, life, and faith. Seeing firsthand how the simple, everyday act of going out to eat can be turned into ministry really impacted me and transformed my thinking about what outreach looks like in a common environment.

On top of forming friendships with the owners and waiters in these restaurants, I also witnessed my parents bringing friends and acquaintances to dine out. These natural settings created a place for our family members to grow closer to new friends, neighbors, and people in our community. We would get to know them better and hear their joys and struggles over chips and salsa or a plate of pork pot stickers. This is where I saw real community and conversation happen among family friends, new believers, and people still trying to figure out what their faith could look like.

While churches and youth buildings are great places to get to know someone and talk about life and faith, many times people outside of the church family seem to feel more comfortable in a setting that is already commonplace for them. No matter what your beliefs or stage of life, everybody needs to eat, and bringing someone out to lunch just to hang out and talk is such a simple, organic thing to do. When we start viewing it as a form of outreach, we can really start to form real relationships and impact the lives of those around us in all sorts of everyday places.

CONNECTING AROUND INTERESTS

As we meet people in our neighborhood, workplace, and community, we need to look for ways in which God might be opening the door for us to reach out to them with his love. One of the most natural ways to build bridges with others is to get involved in the things they are interested in. Christians often expect people to meet us on our home turf, usually in a church building or some type of church-based activity. We certainly believe that it is good to invite people to church, but that's not going to reach everyone. We need to be intentional and take steps to enter into their world as well.

In our neighborhood, we asked what everyone enjoyed doing. This wasn't just a strategy for outreach — their interests really mattered to us! Many of our Christian friends came alongside their neighbors by engaging in the activities their neighbors enjoyed. This might involve doing Creative Memories together, going golfing, seeing a movie, going hunting for the weekend, sharing gardening tips, cooking meals together, attending the same social gatherings and parties, or even doing family trips together and riding the roller coasters at amusement parks. All of these can be natural bridges for building friendships.

It's important that in addition to asking what your neighbors love, you also ask yourself the same question: What do I love doing? Where the answers to these two questions match up, you'll find your natural connection point with other people. While there is nothing wrong with trying something new, if you aren't doing something you love, it won't feel very natural or organic to you or the person you want to spend time with. For example, I love entertaining. I take delight in throwing parties and having people over for special events. These can be neighborhood gatherings, sports parties, small group celebrations, or birthday parties — I'm interested in almost any reason to celebrate. Connecting this way is fun for me. It comes naturally. I also love to listen to people and extend compassion. When I connect in ways that come naturally for me, my outreach is organic.

Kevin's interests are different. He loves to organize events, play sports, and help people learn new skills. He also loves the movies. Through the years I have watched him coach sports teams, play in community sports leagues, organize activities for neighborhood kids, and take our boys' friends out to eat and to the movies. These are ways Kevin connects organically with people.

As a parent, don't forget to ask one additional question: What do my children enjoy? We can also build some great connections when we identify what our children enjoy and invest in those places. Your children's relationships and activities can become organic links to other people in your community. Our boys were interested in sports like soccer, tennis, basketball, and skateboarding, but they were also involved in things like video production and playing in a band (think hard rock, not marching), and we let these be a bridge to families in our city. Your children will have different interests from yours, but the potential for building relationships in your community can be just as rewarding.

CONNECTING THROUGH SMALL GROUPS

Kevin and I had never thought of hosting a small group for the couples in our neighborhood until Rick Warren challenged Christians all over the world to do *The Purpose Driven Life* as a community small group experience.[3] Rick suggested that these groups be comprised of both believers and spiritual seekers. We were a little skeptical at first, at least until we asked our neighbors if they wanted to be part of this book and Bible study. To our surprise, almost everyone we asked said yes.

We partnered with other Christians in our neighborhood and took turns hosting the group. The friends who led the group with us came from a number of different churches, so it did not seem like we were trying to recruit people to our church. Our goal was to learn together. We wanted to see believers grow in faith and give the spiritually curious a safe place to learn about God and ask questions about faith. The Christians in our neighborhood prayed for God to lead this venture, and then we invited our nonchurched friends. For the most part they felt honored to be included and said yes. We all had a great time, and this created an atmosphere where we were able to host other small groups in the future.

Over the past decade there has been a growing effort among Christian leaders and publishers to design small group resources that are friendly to groups of believers and seekers. Some are written explicitly for outreach through community small groups.[4] Some time ago, I came across a helpful resource for people who want to connect with seekers in their community through these types of outreach-oriented small groups. Bob and Betty Jacks started with a simple desire to use their home as a bridge to bring people to Jesus and eventually into the fellowship of the local church, and they wrote a book called *Your Home a Lighthouse: Hosting an Evangelistic Bible Study*.[5] Their example and teaching are helpful for anyone who wants to learn more about hosting and leading an evangelistic small group.

The key is to be creative. Find a way to connect with your community that fits you and meets a need in your neighborhood, town, or city. We have given you some ideas to get the ball rolling, but in the end, for something to be natural and organic, each family needs to discover what works for them in their unique setting. A few years ago a team from our church went to an innovation training day hosted by the Willow Creek Association, several leaders from IDEO, and Gary Hamel.[6] That day, we learned a simple but powerful truth: if you want to succeed more often, you must try new things and be willing to fail more often. Not every attempt you make to connect will be successful, but the only way to ever succeed in engaging your community and being a lighthouse to others is to try. When you find some creative bridges to your community that work, share them with others. If you try to be innovative and your efforts don't bear the fruit you hoped for, don't worry about it. Try something else. Know that God is with you, and he will find a way for his light to shine through you as you step forward in faith, trusting him for the outcome.

BECOMING A LIGHTHOUSE

Try one of these ideas in your home and with your family ...

Youth Culture Study. If you have preteens or teens, consider getting Walt Mueller's book *Youth Culture 101* and studying it. Also spend time talking with your children about how they see their culture and the ways it shapes their view of the world, God, and faith.

What I Love and What You Love. Identify some activity or hobby that one of your neighbors really loves and you also enjoy. Contact them and see if they would like to engage in this activity together. Pray that God will use this natural connection to deepen your friendship and bring the grace of Jesus to this person you care about.

A Reason to Shop and Eat Out. Become a repeat diner or shopper. Identify a place you will frequent for a matter of months. As you shop or dine in this place, get to know the names of the staff and learn some of their personal stories. Pray for God to use you and your family to bring his grace to this place.

Chapter Twelve

Overcoming Outreach Challenges

Kevin

Is not this the kind of fasting I have chosen: to loose the chains of injustice and untie the cords of the yoke, to set the oppressed free and break every yoke? Is it not to share your food with the hungry and to provide the poor wanderer with shelter — when you see the naked, to clothe them, and not to turn away from your own flesh and blood? Then your light will break forth like the dawn, and your healing will quickly appear; then your righteousness will go before you, and the glory of the LORD will be your rear guard.
— *Isaiah 58:6 - 8*

We never know how God will answer our prayers, but we can expect that He will get us involved in His plan for the answer. If we are true intercessors, we must be ready to take part in God's work on behalf of the people for whom we pray.
— *Corrie ten Boom*

Being in the world, **reaching out with God's love, and building bridges to the lost and broken all bring unique challenges. If we** are not careful, the world can influence our children and bring conflict and disunity to our families. Conflicts inevitably arise because there are behaviors and attitudes in the world that we simply can't support, and sometimes we have to push back. If our boundaries aren't clear, we can harm our children or our marriage. Discouragement can set in when we find that not everyone wants to be reached and people we love resist the good news of Jesus and our efforts to show them his love. How do we overcome these challenges?

MAKING AND KEEPING CLEAR BOUNDARIES

One of the most important parenting decisions we faced was how deeply to allow our children to immerse themselves in the lives, homes, and activities of their friends. To guide us, Sherry and I developed a simple philosophy. If our sons were making a difference for Jesus and being influencers, we permitted and encouraged a high level of connection. If a friend was having a harmful impact on any of our sons, we limited the interaction until our son was able to become an influencer again.

This wasn't always easy. Sherry and I had to stay involved in our boys' lives, aware of what their friends were up to, and informed of who was having the most influence. Most of the time we had a strong level of confidence that our sons were having a positive impact for Jesus. Occasionally it was apparent that they were being adversely affected by their relationship with someone, and we helped them navigate those relationships. Sometimes this meant having them back off or cut ties with a negative relationship. We grappled with exactly how to best set healthy boundaries for our kids while still encouraging them to be an influence for Jesus among their friends.

The most important factor in all of this is to stay highly involved in your children's lives. Talk with them often. Know if your children are influencing others for Jesus or if they are being drawn into attitudes and actions that will damage their faith and future. If you believe they are in danger, remember that your first calling and responsibility is to reach your own family members and help them receive and live for Jesus. Clear and appropriate boundaries make this possible.

Jesus set boundaries.[1] He was once asked to go to a city filled with people who wanted him to heal and stay with them. But our Savior was clear that he needed to go on to other towns and preach there. In love, Jesus said, "No." And we need to be okay setting boundaries as well. There are times when the best answer is no, even to something good. Outreach can take a lot out of us, and if we are going to serve faithfully for the long haul, we need to set clear boundaries for ourselves, our children, and those who are not yet followers of Jesus. By setting clear boundaries we model a healthy family life. We also protect ourselves and our family members from being overrun, burned out, and used up.

We tried to help our sons understand what it means to be in the world but not of it. This was particularly tricky from the preteen through the teenage years. One of our boys had a circle of friends that we loved dearly. They spent years in our home, and our hearts' desire was to always have an open house for them, a place where they would always feel welcome. One of the most painful things we had to do as parents was set boundaries with some of these boys when they began getting into more serious kinds of trouble, engaging in activities that could go on their permanent record and cost them for the rest of their lives. We knew that these behaviors could also cost our son if he continued to spend time with his friends.

We had always told our son that he could hang out with these boys as long as we saw that he could make right choices while still being in a close relationship with them. While he was able to be a person of influence for a number of years, during middle school he was caught making some bad choices with these friends, and we had to step in and set some clear boundaries. He was not allowed to hang out with them for a time, and we blocked some of them from being in our home until we felt that things had changed. This was painful for them and for us.

We sought to be as kind as we could. We stayed in contact with their parents, reassuring them of our love and care for their sons. For the most part, the parents understood. We wanted to reach out to these families, but we also felt a strong need to protect our son and keep his faith on track. Closing the door on these struggling teens was one of the hardest things we ever did. But realizing that our own son was at risk forced us to make some tough decisions. With time, some of our son's friends began making better choices, and they are doing well today. Sadly, some of the kids in that group are paying the price of their actions.

Our advice is to allow your children to be connected in the community as long as they are bringing the light and grace of Jesus to others. When it looks like they are being influenced in unhealthy ways, step in and set clear boundaries that will protect their future. This includes setting boundaries for who is welcome in your home and how you interact with others in public. These boundaries can lead to health and long-term ministry for your family.

Saying Not Now

We need to let people know that our home and heart are open to them, but there are also times we reserve for family. Of course, if there is an emergency, we can help at any time. Over the years, we said yes to many opportunities, but we also felt comfortable saying not now. This boundary honored our sons and gave structure to the neighbor kids.

OUR HOME WAS STILL OUR HOME
Nate Harney

Our home was a home to many visitors over the years, but our home was still *our* home. My parents knew they would be having a lot of meetings and parties with families from our church as well as people from our neighborhood and community. For many of these gatherings, my brothers and I just needed a place to hang out that still felt like our home. Instead of kicking us out or sending us to our rooms, my dad and mom created a space in the basement where we could hang out while guests were over. They encouraged us to have fun downstairs during these times and would even knowingly wink at us when they caught us sneaking upstairs on a covert mission to snatch some of mom's awesome Oreo cookie ice cream dessert. I never felt annoyed or displaced by the consistent flow of visitors in our home. My parents always made sure that it still felt like our home.

I also remember my parents setting a lot of boundaries that protected our home from becoming a community center. I watched and learned that it is healthy to open up your home to others. But it is also important to make sure that your kids feel like their home is actually theirs. We were one of the first families in our neighborhood to get a pool. On hot summer days, everyone in the neighborhood wanted to be there. Instead of opening up our home every day of the week to guests, my parents set one day a week as the "neighborhood swim day," when everyone could come and hang out all day. This showed love to our neighbors, but also to us as their sons. Of course, we could invite friends over to swim any day, but the whole neighborhood could not just show up unannounced every day of the week.

This simple action communicated so much to me. I watched as my parents created a space for the neighborhood to come together and have fun but reserved the rest of the time for my brothers and me. In doing this, I saw that my parents cared about reaching our community, but they kept their family their first priority.

Saying No

Through the years there were many times when we simply had to stand our ground and say no. As we mentioned earlier, if one of our sons' friends made poor choices and we were concerned our son might head down that same road, we drew boundaries and said no to that relationship, at least for a time. When Sunday practices were introduced, we gently said no. In our home, while all the kids had "refrigerator rights" to the basement refrigerator, we made sure they knew that did not extend upstairs.[2] I often commented that when our boys and their friends descended on the house, it was like a swarm of locusts devouring everything in their path. It was fine if they wanted to clean out the fridge in the basement, but Sherry needed to know the food she planned for our meals would be there when our family ate. For the most part, people understood and respected our boundaries. Kids from other homes even seemed to like the structure. It was clear to them why we were doing it.

Our oldest son once set a boundary for himself. Zach was in kindergarten, and his teacher was going to read a Halloween story that included witches and other spooky characters. Our son raised his hand and explained that he was not sure if his parents would want him listening to this story. He asked if it would be okay if he sat at a table near the back of the room and did some coloring until the story time was over. The teacher said that would be fine. Another student asked if she could join Zach at the coloring table and was also given permission. As Sherry and I have drawn boundaries for our home and our family with clarity and kindness, all three of our sons have learned to do the same. They have seen that people will respect your convictions if they are expressed with humility and firmness.

CHOOSING BATTLES CAREFULLY

When we live and minister in this world, we will bump up against beliefs and practices that fly in the face of our faith. We will have moments when we need to stand up and resist something that other people in our community do not think is a big deal. Sherry and I have learned to pick our battles carefully and fight gently. Our family lives with strong biblical convictions, but we don't expect nonbelievers to hold the same worldview and philosophy of life as we do. We are not surprised or shocked when a non-Christian does not act like a Christian. When we faced disagreement, and there were plenty of times we did, we sought to follow these four basic guidelines:

1. *Don't become "that family."* There is a Christian family in every community that people find overbearing and obnoxious. They flaunt their faith aggressively and do not show grace in the way they disagree with others. We decided that we were not going to get up on every soapbox and fight every battle that arose. There were some times when other Christians wanted us to join their fight, sign their petition, or ramp up for their cause and we politely said, "No, thank you." We were not going to be crusaders who always had a chip on their shoulder.

2. *Critique from within.* We were committed to raising our concerns from a position of loving service. In our public schools we faced some situations we felt compelled to resist. When one of our sons' sports teams began to schedule practices on Sundays, we made it clear that we did not feel comfortable with our son missing church and family times. We shared our concern, but we did it as parents who consistently supported the coaches, school, and students. We were not just a random, outside voice criticizing the coach. We were committed to helping and serving, and we raised our concern from within. We also talked to the coach directly and did not run to the administration. We wanted to honor him and our relationship with him.

3. *Wait for the big issues.* In all the years of our boys' schooling and participation in community activities, we raised concerns only a handful of times. These were situations when we felt the compromise would be too costly. For instance, we pulled one of our sons out of a sex-education class that was teaching views of sexuality that we felt were inappropriate. But there were only a couple of issues like this that we felt demanded a response. Because we raised concerns from within and did so rarely, we were always met with an understanding ear. In each case our sons were allowed to work around the issues that concerned us.

4. *Extend grace during conflict.* Even when we were disagreeing, we did everything we could not to be disagreeable. We affirmed the leaders, thanked them for their service, and let them know we appreciated all they did, while being clear that we were not able to follow their program. It was always our goal to disagree firmly and still be kind.

These four simple guidelines helped us navigate some of the tougher moments as we connected in our community. Your challenges might be different. Remember to seek guidance in prayer, hold firm to your convictions, but also communicate your disagreements and objections in a way that communicates grace to others.

SERVING OTHERS

We've found that in addition to showing humility in your interactions with others, consistent and humble service is the greatest antidote to the many outreach challenges you will face. This is the way of Jesus. Jesus knew that Thomas would doubt, Peter would deny, Judas would betray, and the rest would run away in his time of need, yet he offered each of them humble service. Our Savior washed his followers' feet as they celebrated the Last Supper, then spoke these words: "Now that I, your Lord and Teacher, have washed your feet, you also should wash one another's feet. I have set you an example that you should do as I have done for you."[3] When we follow in the steps of Jesus, we commit to serving people when they don't deserve it. The truth is that none of us deserves the grace God has freely given. When we recognize how undeserving we are, we are compelled to serve because we are stunned by the magnitude of God's mercy toward us. We serve others because our hearts are filled with gratitude that he gave his life on the cross for us. We love because he first loved us.

The essence of Christian service is not the specific acts we do as much as it is the right condition of our heart. That desire to serve others, motivated by the good news of what Jesus has done for us, can take many different shapes and forms. C. T. Studd once wrote, "If Jesus Christ be God and died for me, then no sacrifice can be too great for me to make for Him."[4] There is nothing too small, too menial, too low for us to do as followers of Christ. Service can be done in many small and ordinary ways. Sherry was known for bringing meals to any family on our street who was dealing with sickness, a birth, or any time of hardship. She had a few simple but delicious meals she would bring and sometimes would give the family a copy of the recipe. People loved this. Acts of service do not have to be extravagant—they must be from the heart, the genuine overflow of God's love for others. We had a family on our street serve us when our dog died. One of the young boys made us a plate of cookies and brought it over. We never forgot it.

Our service should also be creative. We had a group of friends from church that adopted a local creek and cleaned it up on a yearly basis. Buck Creek runs through a park in town where all the community soccer games were played. Whenever we did the creek cleaning day, people from the community would wander over and ask what we were doing. It was a great chance to tell them about our church and why Christians care about the environment.

Some people take the call to service to a whole new level. We know of a group of Christians in Illinois who created a website and formed a 501c3 nonprofit, Cary Grove Neighborhood Life, to serve their community in the name of Jesus.[5] These believers are highly motivated and see their service to their neighbors as a call from God. They hold a "Feed the Hungry" campaign, do special events for seniors, tutor and mentor children in the local schools, practice random acts of kindness, provide supplies for local school teachers, and serve the members of the local fire and police force. Through these connections, doors for the gospel open.[6] Our service can be as simple as helping a neighbor bring in groceries or as industrious as organizing a community-wide service program. The key is that we offer our service in the name of Jesus.

God does not call you to be loved by everyone in your community. He does not call you to serve everyone and meet every need, but he does call you to consistent and humble service. If our home and lives are going to shine with the light of Jesus, we need to intersect in ever-increasing measures right where God has placed us. As we do this, God will use us to bring his love and grace to a broken and hurting world.

BECOMING A LIGHTHOUSE

Try one of these ideas in your home and with your family ...

Boundaries. Ask your kids how you are doing with boundaries in your home. Do they feel that their home is their home? Do they feel displaced? Talk about how you can make your home an inviting place but also help your kids know they are always a priority.

Your Battles. Talk as a family and decide what is worth fighting over. Don't get on every bandwagon. Pick your battles wisely. Be prepared to make a stand and strongly but graciously resist the things you have decided are worth fighting over.

Service Project. Identify as a family one or two acts of service you can offer in your neighborhood, in your apartment complex, on your base, or wherever you live. Pray together and ask God to use these acts of service to build bridges and bring the grace of Jesus to your community.

Concluding Thoughts

Let It Shine!

Why commit to developing a lighthouse home? Hopefully you've found many answers to this question:

- Sharing the love and message of Jesus is our calling.
- Reaching the lost allows us to become more like Jesus.
- Being faithful to God is more important than anything.
- Shining God's light is like no other adventure we will experience.

There are many reasons to engage in organic outreach, but the most important of all is the eternal impact of the message we share. Our mission is one of evangelism, sharing good news that saves people from the eternal consequences of their sins and restores them to a relationship with God through the work of Jesus Christ. There are ways, as we have seen in this book, of doing this naturally and organically so that the message penetrates their hearts and the light of God's truth brings conviction and faith.

SHINING ON A COLD NIGHT

Once, when the temperature was way below freezing, I (Sherry) was out shoveling the driveway and saw my neighbor approaching. It wasn't all that unusual to chat in the driveway with my neighbors, but since it was so cold out, I knew he was coming over for more than a friendly hello. This family was going through some tough challenges, so I asked how he was doing. He was usually a pretty upbeat guy, but he answered me honestly because he knew we cared. "Not so well," he said. We talked for a few minutes, and I told him I would be praying for him.

For the past fourteen years we had been neighbors. We had walked our kids to the school bus stop together and chatted many times. He had been in our home, and we had been in his. We had prayed for and with him. He had been part of small groups that met in our home. Kevin and I had shared our testimonies with him, and he had heard the message of Jesus from both of us. We had gone out to dinner together as families, hung around the pool, laughed until it hurt, and stood to chat in the middle of our cul-de-sac more times than I could count. But this time it felt different.

I had a sense that God wanted me to talk with him about Jesus — just one more time. I shared how God had helped me through the hard times of life and how I knew Jesus wanted to help him as well. I asked if he thought he was ready to take that step of faith and receive the forgiveness and friendship of Jesus. He reflected for a moment, then said yes. And on the frozen ground of our neighborhood, a friend became a brother and asked Jesus to become the leader of his life and forgiver of his sins.

I know that the angels of heaven rejoiced at that moment. I was delighted that God had placed our family on that street as ambassadors of the good news of Jesus. I thanked God that our home was, indeed, a lighthouse of his grace and love. That moment alone made it all worthwhile.

SHINING ON JURY DUTY

When I (Kevin) received a summons for jury duty, I was thankful for the chance to serve my community. I also prayed, "God, if there is someone you want to touch through my life while I serve, here I am. Use me." The first two days of jury duty were uneventful, and we were sent home early. I had no significant interactions. By the third day it looked like we would soon be done, if the two lawyers could come to some kind of agreement. As an officer of the court explained how to get compensated for our time and miles driven, I raised my hand to ask, "Is there something I could sign to donate the money back to the government?" She said there was and told me where I could find the form when we were released.

A friendly gentleman came over to me, sat down, and asked, "Why would you want to give money back to the government?" I explained my sense that they need it more than I do. He found this curious, and we entered a conversation as we waited. We hit it off right away. He owned a small business that was struggling, but he was making ends meet. He happened to be carrying a new age book that I had read as part of some research for writing an article. I asked what he thought of the book, and he said, "Honestly, it's very strange. A friend gave it to me because I am trying to figure out the whole 'God thing.' But it was not helpful at all."

I asked what else he was doing to figure out the God thing, and he said, "I'm just asking a lot of questions." I shared that I was a Christian and also happened to be a pastor. I let him know I would be glad to talk with him about any questions he might have. He asked if we could meet for breakfast sometime, and we set up a date. It turned out he lived in the development next to where I lived. Over the next six months, we met for breakfast every two to three weeks and talked about life, work, his thoughts of going back to school and making a career change, family, golf, and lots of other things. We also talked about God, Jesus, sin, heaven, hell, the Bible, and dozens of other spiritually related topics.

Three different times he seemed open and almost ready to receive Jesus. When I asked if he wanted to take that step, he said he was not quite there yet. Still, he continued to read books I gave him, and he studied the Bible I got for him. After we had been friends and breakfast buddies for over seven months, I sensed that the time was right, and when I asked if he wanted to receive Jesus, he indicated he was now ready. I sat with him as he prayed, and it was amazing to see him grow in his walk with Jesus as we continued to meet for breakfast over the years.

Turning your home into a lighthouse that shines God's love in your neighborhood and community is all about being natural in expressing your faith. Organic outreach is not a program or a method, and we hope it is never a chore or something on a list of things you have to do. It's simply a way to live, love, and serve others in the name of Jesus. As we do this, we discover that God opens opportunities for us to bring the message of his love to others, touching lives. We get to be part of this amazing work.

Our prayer is that you experience the joy of walking with people toward Jesus. First, your children and family members. Then, your neighbors and people in your community. May the God of light shine in and through you for his glory and the good of your community. Amen.

Notes

INTRODUCTION

1. To learn more about helping your church become a force for evangelistic influence in your community and the world, read *Organic Outreach for Churches*.
2. To increase your personal outreach effectiveness and develop natural ways of sharing the good news of Jesus, read *Organic Outreach for Ordinary People*.
3. This book about personal evangelism uses an agricultural motif to help believers discover natural and organic ways to prepare the soil for outreach, plant and water the good news of the gospel, and join in the great harvest of souls God is bringing into his kingdom.
4. This second book in the Organic Outreach series focuses on the local church and uses a motif from human anatomy to help congregations grow their *heart* for the world, focus their *mind* on outreach, get their *hands* dirty and active in service, and train their *mouths* to proclaim the good news of Jesus.
5. Matt. 28:19–20.
6. Acts 1:8.

CHAPTER ONE: LIVING THE GOSPEL IN YOUR HOME

1. Eph. 2:8–9.
2. Rom. 5:8.

CHAPTER TWO: SHARING JESUS WITH YOUR CHILDREN

1. Ps. 139:14.
2. Prov. 22:6 ESV.
3. Charles Swindoll is a great pastor, leader, and prolific author. One of the books we worked with was called *The Strong Family*. Swindoll's insights discussed in this chapter are from that book.
4. The word *exegetical* is about biblical interpretation. In particular, it is about letting the truth and meaning come out of the text rather than imposing our preconceived notions onto the text.
5. Prov. 30:18–19.
6. Ibid.
7. Luke 8:4–8.
8. This is not a recommendation to have a casino night or gamble. It is just part of Kevin's story. In his case it took something over the edge to first draw him in.
9. John 16:7.

10. In *Organic Outreach for Ordinary People*, chapters twelve and thirteen go into great detail about sharing your personal testimony and presenting the gospel.
11. John 3:5–8.

CHAPTER THREE: THE TIMING OF THE SPIRIT

1. Ps. 139:13–16.
2. John 4:4–42.
3. John 3:1–21.
4. Some years ago Kevin wrote a book called *Seismic Shifts*. This book can be used as a study for an individual or a family. It walks through the basics of the Christian faith and is a great tool for a new believer as they take those first and essential steps of faith.

CHAPTER FOUR: REACHING YOUR EXTENDED FAMILY

1. Gal. 5:22.
2. 1 Peter 3:15.
3. The simple presentation of the gospel in this chapter is drawn from a similar one Sherry and I wrote and used in the books *Finding a Church You Can Love* and *Seismic Shifts*.
4. 1 Cor. 15:1–4.
5. Rom. 10:17.
6. I lay out five ways of sharing the gospel in chapter thirteen of *Organic Outreach for Ordinary People*.
7. John 4:4–42.
8. John 3:1–21.
9. Luke 19:1–10.
10. Rom. 5:8.
11. Her website is *www.worknetsolutions.com*.
12. Luke 15:7, 10.

CHAPTER FIVE: THE HOME AS A SAFE HAVEN

1. In chapter six of his book *Surprising Insights from the Unchurched*, Rainer discusses the fact that many people who are looking for a church, including nonbelievers, are very concerned about doctrine and beliefs. This was an insight that surprised Rainer and many other church growth leaders.
2. *winningathome.com*.

CHAPTER SIX: THE HOME AS AN EMERGENCY ROOM

1. Isa. 48:17.
2. E. V. Hill was the pastor of Mount Zion Missionary Baptist Church in Los Angeles for forty-two years, and many called him one of the most influential preachers in America. He passed away in 2003.
3. Gal. 6:2.
4. Exod. 15:26.
5. Randy's book *Making Room for Life* gives many ideas for being available in your neighborhood.

6. Prov. 11:13.
7. Kevin has learned so much about the value of preventative care that he wrote a book, *Leadership from the Inside Out*, for pastors and Christian leaders. Regular and rigorous self-examination can spare leaders from many pitfalls they might face if they live with an unexamined heart.
8. *http://www.hazelden.org/web/public/prev51114.page*.
9. John 1:14.
10. 1 Cor. 6:19.
11. Kevin is so committed to teaching the importance of establishing a rhythm of Sabbath that this topic shows up in most of his books, no matter what the thematic focus.
12. Exod. 20:8–11.

CHAPTER SEVEN: THE HOME AS A PLAYGROUND

1. Gal. 5:22.
2. Phil. 4:4.
3. Acts 16:16–40.
4. Gary's book *Sacred Parenting* has great theology and lots of ideas that will shift your thinking and practice as a parent. We highly recommend it.
5. Chesterton's book *Orthodoxy* is a heavy read and very steeped in the context of his day. At the same time, it is filled with wit and great insight into God and people.
6. The full title of the book is: *The Humor of Christ: A Significant but Often Unrecognized Aspect of Christ's Teaching*.
7. This can be found in C. S. Lewis's book *The Weight of Glory and Other Addresses*.
8. Rom. 8:28.
9. Eccl. 3:1, 4.
10. Neh. 8:10.
11. Luke 17:21.
12. Gary has a great ministry for marriages and families. You can learn more about his work on his website *www.5lovelanguages.com* or in his books, including *The 5 Love Languages* and *The 5 Love Languages for Children*.
13. Ben has served as the chaplain at two Christian colleges (Hope College in Michigan and Westmont College in California). I heard him make this statement at a marriage retreat for our church.

CHAPTER EIGHT: THE HOME AS A PLACE OF PRAYER

1. Luke 15 has three stories that end with rejoicing when the good news transforms a heart and life.
2. John 15:7–8.
3. John 10:3–4.
4. John 1:12–13.
5. Rom. 8:15; Gal. 4:6.
6. Some people believe God got things started and then stepped back from personal involvement in the universe. Deism is the belief in this kind of a god.
7. Phil. 2:6–8.

8. 1 John 4:9–10.
9. Matt. 7:7–11.
10. Mark 1:35.
11. This classic quote is from Leonard Ravenhill.
12. Eph. 2:10.
13. 1 Cor. 3:9.
14. There are many psalms of lament; here are a few: Pss. 3, 4, 5, 6, 22.
15. James 1:5–6.
16. Ps. 32:8.
17. Eph. 6:10–20.
18. John 17:15.
19. 1 John 4:4.
20. 1 Cor. 15:12–57.
21. Mark 12:30.
22. Gal. 5:22–23.
23. For more information on MOPS, see *www.mops.org*. To learn more about Moms in Prayer International, see *www.momsintouch.org*.
24. *Experiencing God* is a wonderful tool for learning to identify where God is at work and join in with him.

CHAPTER NINE: LIGHTHOUSE HOMES

1. John 8:12.
2. John 1:12.
3. 2 Cor. 5:20.
4. 1 Peter 2:9.
5. Rom. 3:23.
6. Rom. 7:15.
7. Matt. 6:24.
8. Mic. 6:8.
9. Matt. 5:9.
10. Gal. 5:22.
11. John 3:19.

CHAPTER TEN: THE SPIRIT AND ATMOSPHERE OF YOUR HOME

1. In *Organic Outreach for Ordinary People*, the entire first chapter is devoted to the central place of love in outreach. In *Organic Outreach for Churches*, the first three chapters focus on the call to love God, love the world, and love the church. You might want to look at these chapters.
2. 1 John 2:15–17, emphasis added.
3. John 3:16, emphasis added.
4. Luke 10:27; Matt. 22:37; Deut. 6:5.
5. John 13:34–35; Rom. 12:10; 1 Thess. 3:12.
6. Matt. 9:35–38.
7. 1 Kings 19:11–12.
8. If you don't have a family budget, you might want to look into a program like Dave Ramsey's Financial Peace University. Learn more at *www.daveramsey.com*.
9. See these programs at *www.biblegateway.com*.

CHAPTER ELEVEN: CONNECTING IN ORGANIC WAYS

1. From Walt Mueller's book, *Youth Culture 101* (Youth Specialties).
2. This seems to be a topic of great passion for Christian parents, and we have been told by people we respect that loving Christian parents will always choose the Christian school option or home schooling. We politely disagree and feel that God can lead people to any schooling option. Our sense of calling to be connected in the public schools could have been very different had the schools been unsafe or had a poor educational track record. We believe each family should take the time to seriously seek God's direction for each child.
3. Rick and the team at Saddleback Church have developed a host of resources for leading a community small group through *The Purpose Driven Life*. You can learn more about these at *www.purposedrivenlife.com* and *www.zondervan .com*.
4. Check out the book *Seeker Small Groups* by Garry Poole. Zondervan has a number of excellent small group series that work well for seekers, including *Interactions*, *Reality Check*, and *Tough Questions*.
5. The book was published in 1987, and over ten years this couple began twenty-five small groups for the purpose of outreach. What a great reminder that seeker small groups have been going on for a long time.
6. This event was led by Gary Hamel, who was named by the *Wall Street Journal* as the world's most influential business thinker. Thomas Kelley, general manager of IDEO, an innovation company (*www.ideo.com*), also presented. For more information on innovation training for the church and Christians, see *www.willowcreek.com*.

CHAPTER TWELVE: OVERCOMING OUTREACH CHALLENGES

1. Mark 1:35 – 39.
2. The book *Refrigerator Rights* by Will Miller explores how we can create connections and restore relationships with people so that we are actually in trusting and sharing relationships.
3. John 13:14 – 15.
4. Studd was a famous cricketer and missionary to China in the late 1800s.
5. Learn more about developing a neighborhood service ministry at *www .carygrove.org*.
6. There are examples of service ideas in both *Organic Outreach for Ordinary People* and *Organic Outreach for Churches* (see chapters 8 and 9).

Organic Outreach for Ordinary People

Sharing Good News Naturally

Kevin G. Harney

Fulfill One of Your Deepest Longings

Organic Outreach for Ordinary People will help you shape a personal approach to passing on the good news of Jesus in natural ways. This is not a system or a program. It's a collection of biblical practices that you can incorporate into your life starting today. On the golf course, over coffee, at your workplace, while taking a walk—anywhere and everywhere—you can become a bearer of grace. This book will help you discover ordinary ways to communicate God's love and the message of salvation—naturally.

Organic Outreach for Churches

Infusing Evangelistic Passion into Your Congregation

Kevin G. Harney

Develop a Culture of Outreach in Your Church

Organic Outreach for Churches provides direction for local congregations to weave evangelism into the fabric of the church. This will not happen accidentally. There is huge spiritual and practical resistance to such changes. But the only way evangelism will become an organic part of a church is when every leader and each member is gripped by a commitment to proclaiming the gospel. This book is a roadmap for pastors and leaders who wish to infuse evangelistic passion into every aspect of their church's life.